Fairytale Cakes

Fairytale Cakes

17 Enchanted Creations

Noga Hitron

LARK
BOOKS

A Division of Sterling Publishing Co., Inc.
New York / London

Editor:

Shoshana Brickman

Art Director:

Matt Shay

Photographer:

Moshe Cohen

Library of Congress Cataloging-in-Publication Data

Hitron, Noga.
  Fairytale cakes : 17 enchanted creations / Noga Hitron. -- 1st ed.
      p. cm.
  Includes bibliographical references and index.
  ISBN 978-1-60059-194-5 (PB-trade pbk. : alk. paper)
  1. Cake decorating. 2. Fairy tales in art. I. Title.
  TX771.2.H58 2008
  641.8'653--dc22

                                    2008015974

10 9 8 7 6 5 4 3 2 1

First Edition

Published by Lark Books, A Division of
Sterling Publishing Co., Inc.
387 Park Avenue South, New York, NY 10016

Text © 2008, Penn Publishing Ltd.
Photography © 2008, Penn Publishing Ltd.
Templates © 2008, Penn Publishing Ltd.

Distributed in Canada by Sterling Publishing,
c/o Canadian Manda Group, 165 Dufferin Street
Toronto, Ontario, Canada M6K 3H6

Distributed in the United Kingdom by GMC Distribution Services,
Castle Place, 166 High Street, Lewes, East Sussex, England BN7 1XU

Distributed in Australia by Capricorn Link (Australia) Pty Ltd.,
P.O. Box 704, Windsor, NSW 2756 Australia

If you have questions or comments about this book, please contact:

Lark Books
67 Broadway
Asheville, NC 28801
828-253-0467

Manufactured in China

ISBN 13: 978-1-60059-194-5

For information about custom editions, special sales, premium and corporate purchases, please contact Sterling Special Sales Department at 800-805-5489 or specialsales@sterlingpub.com.

Note from the Author

childhood is not complete without fairy tales. They lull children to sleep at night and escort them to enchanted dreams. They are the food for young imaginations and the fodder of fantasies. So what could be a more fitting way of celebrating an important childhood event than presenting a beautifully decorated cake based on a favorite fairy tale?

Fairytale Cakes is a collection of cake designs based on the world's best-loved fairy tales. In creating this book, I consulted with fairy tale-lovers of all ages to find out their favorite stories. In developing each cake, I tried to capture one of the story's most evocative scenes. For example, in Little Red Riding Hood, I chose the girl's first fateful meeting with the wolf on her adventurous trip to her Granny's house. As for Rapunzel, the most vivid image I imagined was when she leans out of her tower window, golden locks falling forward.

Designing these cakes was an imaginary adventure that made me feel as if I was part of the story. I hope your decorating experience is just as enchanting, and I hope that you, too, find yourself swept away in the tale. As in all cake decorating projects, the process of making these magical masterpieces is as enjoyable as the result. So roll up your sleeves, roll out your rolled fondant, and delve deep into a favorite childhood tale!

Noga Hitron

Table of Contents

Introduction

elcome to the enchanted world of fairy tale cakes, a collection of cakes depicting memorable scenes from the world's best-loved fairy tales. Each of these cakes recounts a single scene that recalls a complete story. Recreating these scenes using rolled fondant and modeling paste requires a fair amount of time and patience, so plan to have both before you begin. Also make sure you have all the tools and ingredients on hand. If you decide to make changes in your design, perhaps by altering the color of Rapunzel's hair, or the style of the petals in Thumbelina's flower, be sure to account for it when preparing your ingredients. Finally, be sure to have a camera for photographing the finished cake, and take plenty of photographs. Unlike the tales upon which they are based, these cakes surely won't last forever!

Basic Recipes

Cakes

You can use any type of cake you like for these designs, just make sure it is firm and moist. I recommend making the cakes as high as possible—about 3 inches (7.6 cm) or a little more—as this height really shows off the design. If your cake pan is too shallow, line it with parchment paper that extends beyond the rim. The following recipes are fine for making all of the cakes in this book. Use a double batch for The Three Little Pigs (page 110). When baking cakes in a cone pan (see The Snow Queen, page 90), decrease heat by 15 percent, and increase baking time by 15 percent.

Madeira Sponge Cake

Makes one 9 x 3-inch (23 x 7.6 cm) round cake

2 c (500 ml) butter or margarine, room temperature

2 c (400 g) sugar

9 large eggs

4 Tbsp (60 ml) milk or citrus juice

4¼ c (595 g) all-purpose flour

2½ tsp (13 ml) baking powder

1. Preheat oven to 325ºF (160ºC). Grease a 9 x 3-inch (23 x 7.6 cm) round cake pan and line with parchment paper. Make sure the parchment paper extends beyond the top rim of the pan, so that the cake has room to rise.

2. Cream together the butter and sugar with an electric mixer until light and fluffy. Add the eggs one at a time, beating well after each addition. Add the milk and mix. In a separate bowl, sift the flour and baking powder. Add the flour mixture to the creamed mixture, blending with a wooden spoon. Beat until smooth and glossy.

3. Pour the batter into the pan and level with a spatula. Place in the center of the oven and bake for 1¾ to 2 hours, or until a toothpick inserted into the center comes out clean. Cool for 30 minutes in the pan, then turn onto a wire rack until completely cool.

Chocolate Cake

Makes one 9 x 3-inch (23 x 7.6 cm) round cake

2 c (184 g) cocoa

2 c (500 ml) boiling water

1¾ c (300 g) butter or margarine, room temperature

3½ c (700 g) sugar

6 large eggs

3½ c (850 ml) all-purpose flour

4 tsp (20 ml) baking powder

2 tsp (10 ml) rum extract

1. Preheat oven to 350ºF (180ºC). Grease a 9 x 3-inch (23 x 7.6 cm) round cake pan and line with parchment paper. Make sure the parchment paper extends beyond the top rim of the pan, so that the cake has room to rise.

2. Mix the cocoa and water until blended, then set aside for five minutes to cool. Cream together the butter and sugar with an electric mixer until light and fluffy. Add the eggs one at a time, beating well after each addition. Add the rum extract and mix. In a separate bowl, sift the flour and baking powder. Add the flour mixture to the creamed mixture, alternating with the cocoa mixture, and beating thoroughly after each addition.

3. Pour the batter into the pan and level with a spatula. Place the cake in the center of the oven and bake for 50 minutes, or until a toothpick inserted in the center comes out clean. Cool for 30 minutes in the pan, then turn onto a wire rack until completely cool.

Fruity Cake

Makes one 9 x 3-inch (23 x 7.6 cm) round cake

1¾ c (300 g) butter or margarine, room temperature

4 c (875 g) brown sugar

6 large eggs

1 c (250 ml) oil

2 tsp (10 ml) vanilla extract

6 c (840 grams) all-purpose flour

2 tsp (10 ml) salt

2 tsp (10 ml) baking soda

4 tsp (20 ml) cinnamon

2 29-oz (810 g) cans peach or pear halves in light syrup

½ c (125 ml) coarsely ground pecans

1. Preheat oven to 350ºF (180ºC). Grease a 9 x 3-inch (23 x 7.6 cm) round cake pan and line with parchment paper. Make sure the parchment paper extends beyond the top rim of the pan, so that the cake has room to rise.

2. Cream together the butter and sugar with an electric mixer until light and fluffy. Add the eggs, oil, and vanilla extract, and beat thoroughly. In a separate bowl, combine the flour, salt, baking soda, and cinnamon. Drain the peaches, reserving the syrup from one can. Add the flour mixture to the creamed mixture, alternating with the peaches, and beating thoroughly after each addition. Add the pecans and mix thoroughly.

3. Pour the batter into the pan and level with a spatula. Place the cake in the middle of the oven and bake for 50 minutes, or until a toothpick inserted into the center comes out clean. Pour over the reserved syrup while the cake is still warm. Cool for one hour in the pan, then turn onto a wire rack until completely cool.

Cookie Dough

Makes about 25 large cookies

1 c (226 g) unsalted butter, cold

1 c (200 g) sugar

3 large eggs

1 tsp (5 ml) pure vanilla extract

3½ c (490 g) all-purpose flour

1. Cream together the butter and sugar with an electric mixer until light and fluffy. Add the eggs one at a time, beating thoroughly after each addition. Add the vanilla and mix well on low speed. Add the flour one cup at a time, mixing well after each addition. Mix just until a ball is formed, taking care not to overmix. The dough should be a little stiff, but not sticky. If it becomes too stiff, add a little water.

2. Divide the dough into two balls, wrap each ball in plastic wrap, and refrigerate until ready to use.

3. Before cutting out cookies, transfer cookie dough to a piece of parchment paper and flatten with your hands. Cover with another sheet of parchment paper and roll out to a thickness of ¼-inch (0.6 cm) thick.

Buttercream

This sweet spread is used to cover the cake, and provide a smooth surface for applying the rolled fondant. You can use jam, chocolate spread, marzipan, or ready-made buttercream. To make your own buttercream, follow the recipe below.

Makes 3 cups (750 ml)

1 c (226 g) butter or margarine, room temperature

1 tsp (5 ml) vanilla extract

4 c (460 g) sifted confectioners' sugar

2 Tbsp (30 ml) milk

1. Cream the butter with an electric mixer. Add the vanilla and mix well. Sift the sugar into the bowl, one cup at a time, while beating on medium speed. Scrape the sides and bottom of the bowl often. When all the sugar has been added, the icing will appear dry. Add the milk and beat on medium speed until light and fluffy.

2. Use immediately or transfer to an airtight container and refrigerate for up to two weeks. Re-whip before using.

Rolled Fondant

Also known as sugarpaste, plain rolled fondant is white or off-white. Ready-made varieties are tasty, and easy to use, but if you'd like to make it yourself, follow the recipe below.

Makes 2 lb (900 g)

1 Tbsp (15 ml) unflavored gelatin

3 Tbsp (45 ml) cold water

½ c (125 ml) liquid glucose

1 Tbsp (15 ml) glycerin

2 Tbsp (30 ml) solid vegetable shortening

8 c (920 g) sifted confectioners' sugar

1. Put the gelatin in the water and let stand until thick. Place the gelatin mixture in the top of a double boiler and gently heat until dissolved. Add the glucose and glycerin, and mix well. Stir in the shortening and just before it melts completely, remove from the heat. Allow the mixture to cool slightly.

2. Place 4 cups of confectioners' sugar in a bowl and make a well. Pour the gelatin mixture into the well and stir, mixing in the sugar until the stickiness disappears. Knead in the remaining sugar until the mixture doesn't stick to your hands.

3. Tightly wrap in plastic and store in an airtight container until ready to use. Place in a cool, dry place. Do not refrigerate or freeze.

Modeling Paste
(Rolled Fondant with CMC)

Adding a thickening material to rolled fondant makes it malleable for modeling. Carboxyl Methyl Cellulose (CMC) and tragacanth gum are two types of edible thickening agents that are used for this purpose. CMC is cheaper than tragacanth gum, and can be stored for a longer period of time.

Makes 1 lb (454 g)

Cornstarch, for dusting

2 tsp (10 ml) CMC or gum tragacanth

1 lb (454 g) rolled fondant

1. Dust a dry surface with the cornstarch and sprinkle the CMC overtop. Place the rolled fondant on the CMC and knead until smooth. Store in an airtight container for at least one hour before use.

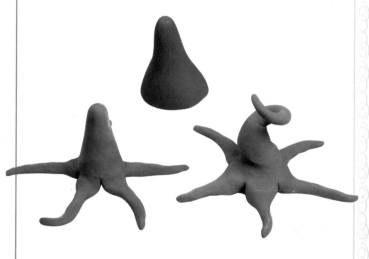

Royal Icing

This sweet mixture is used to hold pieces of modeling paste together, and to affix figures onto the cake. It can be made with meringue powder or fresh egg whites.

Makes 1½ c (375 ml)

1 Tbsp meringue powder

2 Tbsp water

1½ c (175 g) sifted confectioners' sugar

1 Tbsp water

1. Dissolve the meringue powder in the water, and stir until completely blended and free of lumps. Add the confectioners' sugar and beat on low speed for 10 minutes, until the mixture has the consistency of thick cream or syrup.

2. To test the consistency, draw a knife through the icing and count to 10. If the mark disappears by the time you reach 10, you have the right consistency. Add water to thin, or confectioners' sugar to thicken. Use immediately or transfer to an airtight container and store at room temperature for up to two weeks.

Tools

You'll use a variety of tools when decorating cakes with rolled fondant and modeling paste. Some of these items are likely to be found in your kitchen; others are unique to the craft. You should be able to find everything you need at specialty stores, through catalogs, or online.

Bone tools are used for indenting modeling paste and rolled fondant.

Cake boards are used for presenting the decorated cake. They come in a variety of shapes and styles, and may be covered with decorated paper, foil, ribbon, or rolled fondant.

Cake rounds are used for tracing large circles onto rolled fondant. You can also trace the edge of a large plate, or the inside rim of a springform pan.

Cutters of various shapes and sizes are used to make flowers, leaves, circles, hearts, and other shapes. You may also use cups, plates, or templates.

Decorating bag and tip is used for piping royal icing. Make your own decorating bags out of rolled parchment paper, or purchase ready-made bags.

Dry spaghetti and wooden skewers are used for supporting figures. Dry spaghetti is safer than wooden skewers, but some features require the extra stability provided by skewers. In such cases, make sure you trim the sharp end of the skewer. Remove all non-edible supports before serving the cake.

Fine paintbrushes are used to apply water for affixing modeling paste and for painting on gel food color.

Floral wire is used to affix items such as leaves and petals to cakes.

Leaf veiner is used to press vein patterns onto leaves.

Marking tools are used for marking gentle lines on modeling paste and rolled fondant.

Open-curve crimper, also called a "single closed scallop crimper", is used to create textured trim around the edges of cakes.

Pieces of sponge are useful for supporting figures as they dry.

Pizza cutter is used to trim the rolled fondant. Though a sharp knife can also be used, the rolling edge of the pizza cutter allows for a smoother cut.

Rolling pins are used for rolling out modeling paste and rolled fondant. Textured rolling pins are used to create textured surfaces, such as stripes or bricks.

Sharp knives with straight edges are used to cut modeling paste and rolled fondant. Use a knife with a serrated edge to trim cakes.

Sharp scissors may be used to cut modeling paste, for example, to make a pointed crown.

Silicone molds are used to form small objects such as sculpted faces.

Toothpicks are perfect for making small marks or holes. They are also used as supports, so be sure to use high quality toothpicks that don't splinter.

Basic Techniques

Adding color

I recommend using gel food color to tint rolled fondant, modeling paste, and royal icing, as it is nontoxic and doesn't leave an aftertaste. It comes in a wide variety of colors, which can be blended to create an even wider palette of colors.

When tinting, dip a toothpick into the food color and add to the rolled fondant or modeling paste. Knead until evenly blended, adding a little gel at a time, until you have the desired shade. You may want to wear gloves when kneading as the color can stain your hands.

The addition of CMC causes color to fade, so you may need more food color to tint modeling paste than you do to tint rolled fondant.

If possible, add food color to the rolled fondant before adding the CMC, as it will be easier to knead.

Working with rolled fondant and modeling paste

Read the instructions from start to finish before starting to model any of the figures in these cakes. Modeling paste dries quickly, and it is best to affix the pieces very soon after shaping them. This means you may not necessarily want to shape all the pieces first and then assemble them, but rather affix the pieces to each other as they are shaped.

Always work on a dry surface that is lightly covered with cornstarch.

The quantities suggested in this book are generous, because working with small quantities is difficult, especially when adding color. Furthermore, it's much better to be left with too much rolled fondant or modeling paste than too little.

If the rolled fondant you are working with is too hard, try heating it in the microwave for a few seconds. Do not overheat!

If your modeling paste isn't stable enough or if you are working with figures that are particularly tall or thin, add a little more CMC.

Tightly wrap any leftover rolled fondant and modeling paste. When stored in an airtight container and kept in a cool, dry place, it can last for several months. Do not refrigerate or freeze.

If you are working with a really thin sheet of rolled fondant, cover it with plastic cling wrap as you work, to stop the fondant from hardening while you work.

If you find it hard to make a single sausage to surround a cake or cake board, try lining up two or three sausages end-to-end.

Preparing and covering the cake

Line your cake pan with parchment paper before pouring in the batter. This helps the cake come out smoothly, and with a minimal amount of crumbling. Also, by allowing the parchment paper to extend beyond the rim of the pan, your cake will have more room to rise.

Level your cake with a sharp serrated knife and turn it upside down before applying rolled fondant.

In most cases, it's best to decorate your cake directly on the cake board. If you want to continue working on your work surface, place the cake on a cake round or thick piece of cardboard. This makes transferring the cake to the cake board much easier.

To determine the area of rolled fondant you'll need to cover your cake, measure the sides and the top of the cake across the center. Add about 1 inch (2.5 cm) on either side for trimming. For example, a 10 x 3-inch (25 x 7.6 cm) round cake will require a piece of rolled fondant that is about 18 inches (46 cm) in diameter.

When covering a cake, roll out the rolled fondant to a thickness of about ¼ inch (0.6 cm). Lay a rolling pin under the middle of the rolled fondant and carefully lift it above the center of the cake. Gently lay one half of the rolled fondant onto the cake, so that it covers one side of the cake completely. Lay the other half of the fondant over the other side of the cake, and gently smooth with your hands, starting in the middle and working your way around the sides.

Trim away excess rolled fondant around the edges of the cake with a pizza cutter or sharp knife.

Store decorated cakes in a dry, cool place that is away from direct heat or sunlight. Do not refrigerate or freeze.

Please note: Non-edible supports such as wooden skewers, dry spaghetti, and toothpicks are used in some cakes. Please remove all non-edible supports before serving the cake.

Hansel and Gretel

 **ansel and Gretel lived with their widower father in a small cottage by the forest.** One day, an evil witch plotted to get the children lost in the forest. Her first effort to lead them astray failed, because Hansel was clever and left a trail of rocks which they followed home. The witch's next attempt was successful, however, as this time Hansel left a trail of breadcrumbs that was eaten by birds. Hansel and Gretel were lost, hungry, and tired when they came upon a house made of candy. The house actually belonged to the witch, who trapped the children inside, and put Hansel in a cage. Gretel was the clever one this time. She pushed the witch into a hot oven and freed Hansel from his cage. The children discovered valuable treasures in the witch's house, found their way home, and lived happily ever after.

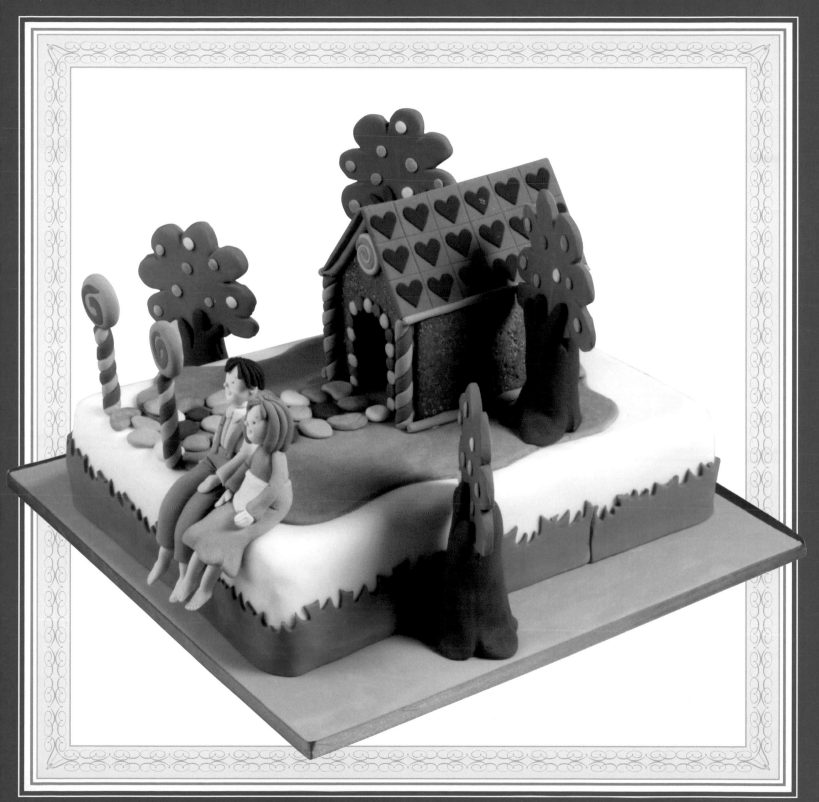

Materials

1 batch cookie dough (page 11)

3 lb 15 oz (1.8 kg) modeling paste (page 12), divided and tinted to make:

    6¼ oz (177 g) bright orange

    2½ oz (71 g) red

    3 oz (85 g) pink

    1 oz (28 g) light orange

    1 lb (454 g) dark green

    1 lb 3 oz (549 g) dark brown

    ¾ oz (21 g) yellow

    3 oz (85 g) dark turquoise

    2½ oz (71 g) light blue

    3 oz (85 g) skin color

    2½ oz (71 g) light purple

    2½ oz (71 g) lilac

    ½ oz (14 g) white

    ½ oz (14 g) light brown

1 batch royal icing (page 13), tinted brown

3 lb 3 oz (1.44 kg) rolled fondant (page 12), divided and tinted to make:

    1 lb (454 g) light green

    2 lb (900 g) white

    3 oz (85 g) light brown

14 x 14-inch (36 x 36 cm) square cake board

9 x 13 x 3-inch (23 x 33 x 7.6 cm) rectangle cake (pages 9-10)

1 batch buttercream (page 11)

Tools

Rolling pin

Small sharp knife

Marking tool

Small heart cutter

Fine paintbrush

Decorating bag and tip

Wooden skewers

Toothpicks

Bone tool

Dry spaghetti

Pieces of sponge

Pizza cutter

Serrated knife

Instructions

The house

1. Preheat oven to 350°F (180°C). Roll out the cookie dough and cut out walls using the template on page 122. Bake for about six to eight minutes, or until golden. Cool for about 30 minutes on the cookie sheet, then transfer to a wire rack to cool completely (Figure 1). Make one side of the roof by rolling out 3 oz (85 g) of bright orange modeling paste and cut out a 3 x 6-inch (7.6 x 15.4 cm) rectangle. Mark 18 squares on the rectangle using the marking tool. Thinly roll out ½ oz (14 g) of red modeling paste and cut 18 hearts using the heart cutter (Figure 2). Affix a heart to the center of each square. Repeat to make the other side of the roof and set aside to dry for six hours. Assemble the walls of the house using royal icing, and set aside to dry for three hours. When the walls are stable, affix the roof and set aside to dry for three hours.

2. Roll ¼ oz (7 g) of pink modeling paste into a small sausage. Roll a similar sausage with light orange modeling paste and press together. Coil the sausages into a circle (Figure 3). Affix on the front of the house, at the top. Roll 1 oz (28 g) of pink modeling paste into a 20-inch (51.2 cm) sausage and cut into four even sections. Affix a section along the top and bottom of each side of the house. Roll ½ oz (14 g) of pink modeling paste into a 12-inch (30.7 cm) sausage and cut in half. Affix both halves just under the roof on the front of the house. Roll ¼ oz (7 g) of pink modeling paste into a small sausage. Roll a similar sausage with red modeling paste and twist together. Affix along the corners at the front of the house. Set aside to dry for three hours.

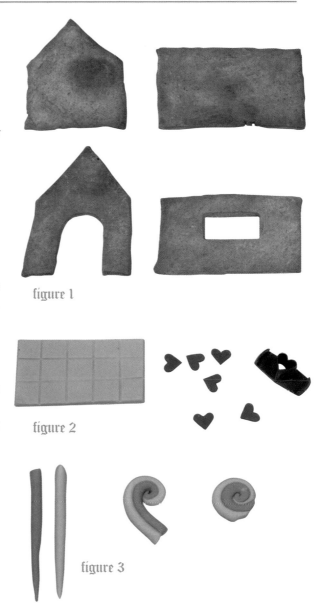

figure 1

figure 2

figure 3

The trees

3. Roll out 2 oz (57 g) of dark green modeling paste and cut a treetop using the template on page 123. Carefully insert a skewer into the bottom of the treetop, and set aside to dry for three hours. Roll 4 oz (114 g) of dark brown modeling paste into a thick cylinder and shape into a trunk. Make a horizontal cut at the top that is wide enough to support the treetop, and shape branches at the front and back. Make candy fruit by rolling and flattening several small balls of modeling paste in various colors. To assemble the tree, press the skewer extending from the treetop into the trunk, and affix the branches and candy fruit (Figure 4). Make three more trees and set aside to dry for three hours.

The lollipops

4. Roll ½ oz (14 g) of pink modeling paste into a ball and flatten. Roll a little bit of bright orange modeling paste into a thin sausage and coil onto the face of the flattened pink ball. Roll gently to integrate. Roll ¼ oz (7 g) of light orange modeling paste into a thin sausage. Roll the same amount of yellow modeling paste into a thin sausage and twist the two sausages together. Insert a wooden skewer into the twisted orange and yellow sausage, ensuring that some of the skewer extends from both the top and bottom of the sausage. Press the flattened pink ball onto the top of the skewer (Figure 5). Repeat to make a second lollipop and set aside to dry for six hours.

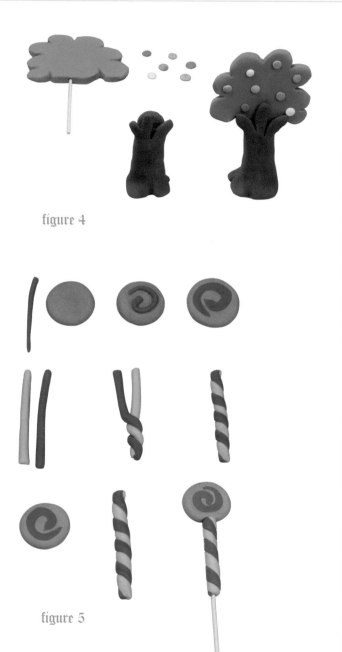

figure 4

figure 5

figure 6

Hansel

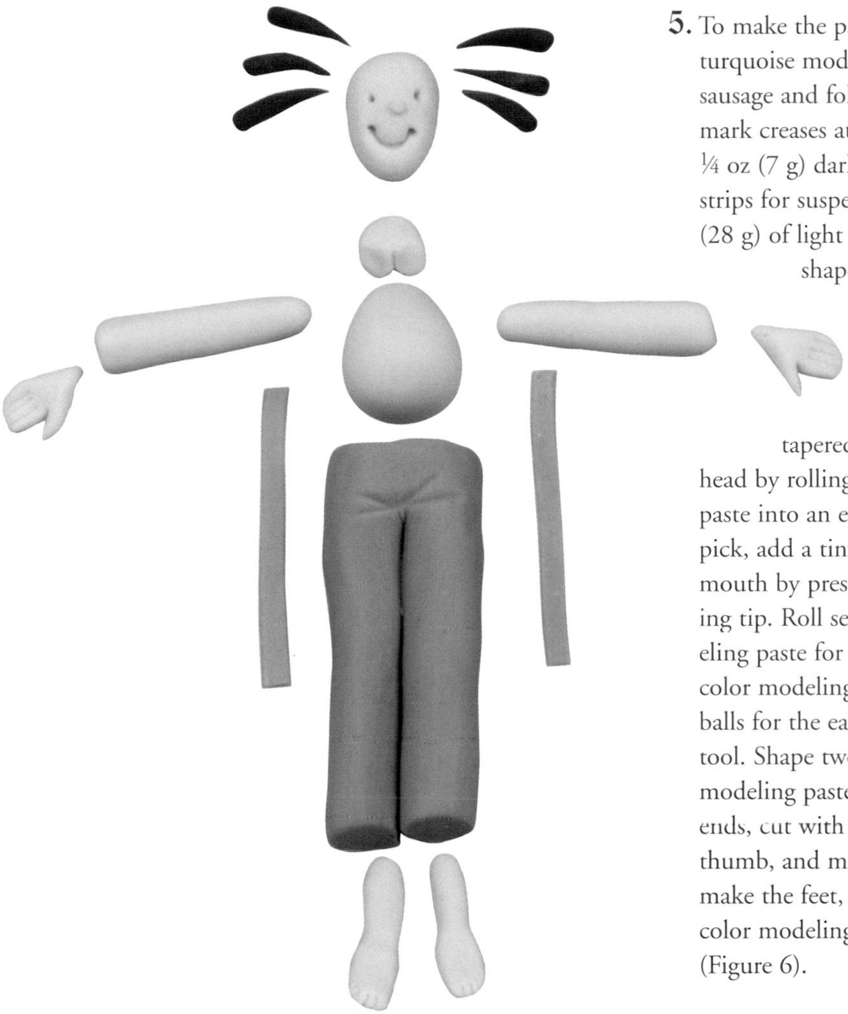

5. To make the pants, roll 2½ oz (71g) of dark turquoise modeling paste into a 4-inch (10 cm) sausage and fold in half. Square off the top and mark creases at the top of each leg. Thinly roll out ¼ oz (7 g) dark turquoise modeling paste and cut strips for suspenders. To form the shirt, roll 1 oz (28 g) of light blue modeling paste into a egg shape. Shape ¼ oz (7 g) of light blue modeling paste into a ball, flatten, and trim along one side to form a bow tie. Roll 1 oz (28 g) of light blue modeling paste into two tapered cylinders for the sleeves. Make the head by rolling 1 oz (28 g) of skin color modeling paste into an egg shape. Mark eyes with a toothpick, add a tiny ball for the nose, and mark the mouth by pressing in the wide end of a decorating tip. Roll several sausages of dark brown modeling paste for the hair. Roll a small ball of skin color modeling paste for the neck and two tiny balls for the ears. Indent the ears with the bone tool. Shape two small teardrops of skin color modeling paste for the hands. Flatten the wider ends, cut with the sharp knife to separate the thumb, and make shallow cuts to form fingers. To make the feet, roll two small sausages of skin color modeling paste and bend at the ankles (Figure 6).

6. Assemble the figure on an elevated surface, such as an inverted cake pan. Begin by folding the pants at the knees. Insert a piece of dry spaghetti into the top of the pants, leaving enough extending from the top to provide support through to the head. Press the shirt, bow tie, and neck onto the spaghetti. Mark a seam down the front of the

shirt with the marking tool, and affix the suspenders on either side of the seam. Press on the head and affix the hair and ears. Affix the sleeves on either side of the body, and bend gently at the elbows. Affix the hands and feet, and place pieces of sponge under the feet for support. Set aside to dry for six hours.

Gretel

7. To make the skirt, roll 2 oz (57 g) of light purple modeling paste into a 3-inch (7.6 cm) cylinder. Press down on the front to flatten slightly and make it narrower at the top to form a waist. Widen the bottom by pressing in with your fingers to form the hem. Shape the shirt by rolling 1 oz (28 g) of lilac modeling paste into an egg shape. Roll 1 oz (28 g) of lilac modeling paste into two tapered cylinders for sleeves. Thinly roll out the white modeling paste and cut a belt and apron. Make Gretel's head, hands, and feet using the same techniques as for Hansel. Roll longer sausages of light brown modeling paste for the hair (Figure 7).

8. Assemble the figure on an elevated surface, such as an inverted cake pan. Begin by folding the skirt at the knees. Insert a piece of dry spaghetti into the top of the skirt, leaving enough extending from the top to provide support through to the head. Press the shirt and neck onto the spaghetti. Wrap the belt and apron around the waist. Press the head onto the spaghetti and affix the hair.

Affix the sleeves on either side of the body, and bend gently at the elbows. Affix the hands and feet, and place pieces of sponge under the feet for support. Set aside to dry for six hours.

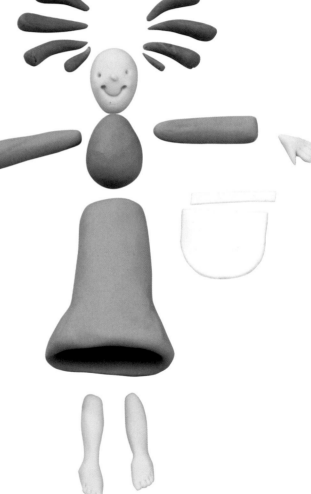

figure 7

Cake and cake board

9. Thinly roll out the light green rolled fondant and cover the cake board. Trim the edges with the pizza cutter and set aside to dry for three hours. Level the cake with the serrated knife and turn it upside down onto a flat surface. Spread buttercream generously on the top and sides. Roll out the white rolled fondant, wrap the cake, and trim the edges. Transfer to the cake board and position in the middle. Roll 8 oz (227 g) of dark green modeling paste into a strip that measures 2 x 44 inches (5 x 112.6 cm). Straighten one long edge and cut the other long edge in a jagged manner so that it resembles grass. Affix around the bottom of the cake. To make the base for the house, thinly roll out the light brown rolled fondant. Cut out a shape with wavy sides, and affix on the surface of the cake. Affix the house and trees on the cake. Roll several small balls of modeling paste in various colors, flatten, and affix in a path at the front of the house, and as a trim around the door and window. Position the lollipops on either side of the path and affix Hansel and Gretel at the edge of the cake. Set aside to dry for three hours.

Remove all non-edible supports before serving the cake.

The Frog Prince

 **young princess lost her favorite golden ball down a well.** A funny-looking frog offered to retrieve the ball if the princess would allow him to eat from her plate and sleep in her room. The princess agreed, and the frog fetched the ball. Delighted by the return of her toy, the princess forgot all about her promise and ran off to play in the palace. Later that day, when the princess sat down to lunch with the king, the frog appeared and reminded the princess of her promise. The king told his daughter that promises must be kept, so with great reluctance, the princess allowed the frog to eat from her plate and sleep in her room. The frog was sad, because he knew the princess was just obeying the king. The princess's heart which softened when she saw the sad frog. She gave him an apologetic kiss and he immediately transformed into a handsome prince.

Materials

2 lb 5½ oz (1.1 kg) modeling paste (page 12), divided and tinted to make:

- 5 oz (142 g) white
- 5 oz (142 g) yellow
- 1 lb (454 g) dark green
- ¾ oz (21 g) red
- ¼ oz (7 g) black
- 3 ½ oz (100 g) light green
- 6 oz (170 g) pink
- 2 oz (57 g) skin color

Blue, brown, and red gel food color

Gold luster powder

1 batch royal icing (page 13)

9 x 3-inch (23 x 7.6 cm) round cake (pages 9-10)

1 batch buttercream (page 11)

2 lb 9 oz (1.1 kg) rolled fondant (page 12), divided and tinted to make:

- 2 lb (900 g) white
- 9 oz (255 g) turquoise

12-inch (30.5 cm) round cake board

Tools

Rolling pin

Small flower cutter

Toothpicks

Pieces of sponge

Bone tool

Fine paintbrush

Small sharp knife

Marking tool

Dry spaghetti

Sharp scissors

Decorating bag and tip

Serrated knife

Pizza cutter

Open-curve crimper

7-inch (17.8 cm) cake round or large plate

Instructions

Flowers and leaves

1. Very thinly roll out ⅛ oz (4 g) of white modeling paste. Cut a flower with the flower cutter and roll over each petal with a toothpick to frill. Lay the flower on a piece of sponge and press in at the middle with the bone tool. Make a center for the flower by rolling a tiny ball of yellow modeling paste. Indent the ball with the bone tool, and affix in the middle of the flower. Make a leaf by rolling ¼ oz (7 g) of dark green modeling paste into a narrow strip. Fold the strip in half lengthwise, then fold widthwise and bend the tips (Figure 1). Repeat to make 32 flowers and 12 leaves. Set aside to dry for three hours.

The frog

2. Roll 12½ oz (354 g) of dark green modeling paste into a rounded cone. Cut a crescent about halfway up from the bottom and shape into a wide smile. Use a toothpick to mark two nostrils just above the mouth (Figure 2). Roll the red modeling paste into a flat strip, shape into a tongue, and affix inside the mouth. Form eyes by rolling the remaining dark green modeling paste into two egg shapes, and affix above the nostrils. Add small balls of yellow modeling paste and smaller balls of black modeling paste. Form each leg by rolling 1 oz (57 g) of light green modeling paste into a 4-inch (10 cm) sausage. To make each webbed foot, roll ¾ oz (21 g) of light green modeling paste into a ball, flatten, and pinch four lines along the top. Fold each leg in the middle and position on either side of the body. Affix a webbed foot in front of each leg and set aside to dry for three hours.

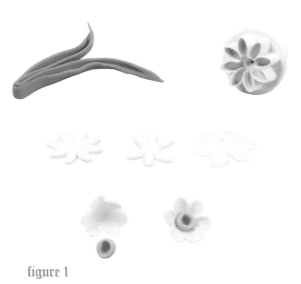

figure 1

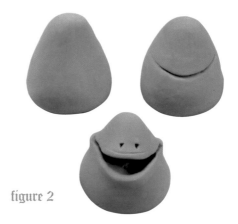

figure 2

The princess

3. To make the dress, roll 5½ oz (155 g) of pink modeling paste into a rounded cone. Form a waist by narrowing the cone about three-quarters of the way up from the bottom. Gently pinch the top to form a neckline, and press in at the sides to form grooves for the arms. Mark pleats in the skirt with the marking tool, and shape the modeling paste between the pleats to form the flowing bottom of the skirt (Figure 3). To make each glove, roll ½ oz (14 g) of white modeling paste into a sausage, and gently pinch to form an elbow and wrist. Flatten the area below the wrist to make a hand, cut with the sharp knife to separate the thumb, and make shallow cuts to form fingers (Figure 4). Repeat to make a second glove. To make the sleeves, roll a little pink modeling paste into two small cones, and indent the wider end with the bone tool. Roll a tiny sausage of pink modeling for decorating the neckline. Form upper arms by rolling two small cylinders of skin color modeling paste. Roll 1 oz (28 g) of skin color modeling paste into an egg shape for the head. Mark eyes with a toothpick and add a tiny ball for the nose. Make the neck by shaping a little skin color modeling paste into a teardrop. Flatten and shape the wider end so that it fits into the neckline of the dress. Roll 1½ oz (42 g) of yellow modeling paste into long sausages for the hair (Figure 5).

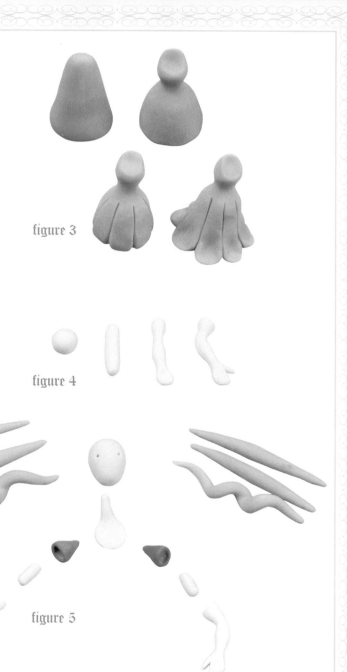

figure 3

figure 4

figure 5

4. To assemble the figure, insert a piece of dry spaghetti into the top of the dress, leaving enough extending from the top to provide support through to the head. Press the neck onto the spaghetti and affix the pink trim at the neckline. Affix the sleeves at either side of the body, and insert a toothpick to support the arm that extends outwards. Affix the arms and gloves in the desired position and support with pieces of sponge. Press the head onto the spaghetti, paint on facial features with the gel food color, and affix the hair. Set aside to dry for six hours.

Gold ball and crowns

5. Roll 1½ oz (42 g) of yellow modeling paste into three balls of various sizes. Leave the largest ball as is. Shape the medium ball into a crown by pressing your thumb into the top of the ball. Draw the top edge upwards and cut six triangular points with sharp scissors. Shape the smallest ball into a crown using the same technique, but cut just four triangular points along the top. Set aside for 30 minutes. Mix the gold luster powder with a little water, and paint the ball and crowns. Set aside to dry for 3 hours. Affix the smaller crown to the princess and the larger crown to the frog using a little royal icing.

Cake and cake board

6. Level the cake with the serrated knife and turn it upside down onto a flat surface. Spread buttercream generously on the top and sides. Set aside ½ oz (14 g) of white rolled fondant and roll out the rest. Wrap the cake and trim the edges with the pizza cutter. Use the open-curve crimper to crimp along the top edge of the cake. Transfer to the cake board and position in the middle. Roll 7 oz (198 g) of turquoise rolled fondant into a 24-inch (61 cm) sausage. Cut the sausage into six even pieces and affix around the base of the cake, leaving a 1-inch (2.5 cm) space between each sausage. Knead together the remaining turquoise rolled fondant with the remaining white rolled fondant until the colors are swirled, but not blended. Cut out a circle using the cake round and affix on top of the cake. Affix the princess, frog, gold ball, and a few flowers on the top of the cake. Affix a few flowers between each section of the turquoise trim, and arrange the remaining flowers and leaves around the top edge of the cake. Set aside to dry for three hours.

Remove all non-edible supports before serving the cake.

Aladdin

n adventurous boy named Aladdin met an evil magician. The magician promised Aladdin great wealth if he would crawl into a tunnel and retrieve a lamp. Aladdin agreed and entered the tunnel. He found a lamp, a magic carpet, and countless other treasures. Aladdin realized the magician was up to no good and refused to hand over the lamp. The furious magician trapped Aladdin in the tunnel, but the clever boy soon discovered that rubbing the lamp released a wish-granting genie. By wishing, Aladdin escaped from the tunnel and achieved great wealth. He traveled the world on his magic carpet, wooed a beautiful princess, and built a marvelous palace.

Materials

1 teaspoon (5 ml) CMC

2 lb 8½ oz (1.1 kg) modeling paste (page12),
divided and tinted to make:

   7 oz (198 g) red

   13½ oz (382 g) white

   1½ oz (42 g) turquoise

   1½ oz (42 g) skin color

   1 oz (28 g) yellow

   1 oz (28 g) orange

   ½ oz (14 g) black

   7½ oz (300 g) light brown

   3½ oz (100 g) dark brown

   3½ oz (100 g) sand color

Gold luster powder

1 batch royal icing (page 13)

Black gel food color

2 lb 14 oz (1.3 kg) rolled fondant (page 12),
divided and tinted to make:

   14 oz (396 g) green

   2 lb (900 g) turquoise

   8 oz (227 g) white

9 x 13 x 3-inch (23 x 33 x 7.6 cm) rectangle cake
(pages 9-10)

1 batch buttercream (page 11)

10 x 14-inch (25.6 x 36 cm) rectangle cake board

Tools

Rolling pin

Pizza cutter

Cardboard cylinder (from a roll of paper towels),
cut in half lengthwise

Small sharp knife

Marking tool

Fine paintbrush

Bone tool

Decorating bag and tip

Toothpicks

Dry spaghetti

Large flower cutter

Serrated knife

Instructions

The carpet

1. Add the CMC to the red modeling paste to make it particularly stiff. Set aside a tiny ball of the modeling paste for later, and roll out the rest. Cut into a 6 x 8-inch (15.2 x 20.3 cm) rectangle using the pizza cutter. Arrange the cylinder halves so that they are parallel, about 2 inches (5 cm) apart. Lay the carpet on top of the cylinders so that it takes on their curves, and set aside to dry for nine hours. Mix the gold luster powder with a little water and paint a design along the edges (Figure 1). Set aside to dry for three more hours. Prepare a base for the carpet by molding 8 oz (227 g) of white modeling paste into a large cloud shape. Set aside to dry for three hours.

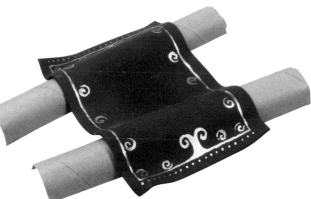

figure 1

Aladdin

2. To make the pants, roll 5 oz (142 g) of white modeling paste into a teardrop. Flatten the back, and make a vertical cut extending from the middle of the teardrop to the bottom. Shape the modeling paste on either side of the cut into a ballooning pant leg, and mark creases with the marking tool (Figure 2). Roll ¼ oz (7 g) of turquoise modeling paste into a ball and flatten to form the belt. Roll ½ oz (14 g) of turquoise modeling paste into a rounded egg shape for the shirt. Roll the remaining turquoise modeling paste into two elongated cones for the sleeves, and indent each sleeve at the wide end with the bone tool. To make the hands, shape two small

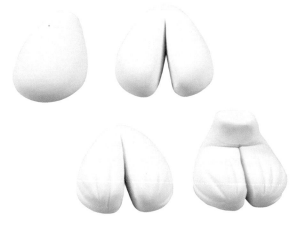

figure 2

teardrops of skin color modeling paste. Flatten the wider ends, cut with the sharp knife to separate the thumb, and make shallow cuts to form fingers. Roll out a little white modeling paste and cut a small triangle for the shirt front. Make shirt front decorations by rolling two thin sausages of yellow modeling paste, and forming a small ball with the red modeling paste set aside previously. Shape the orange modeling paste into two teardrops for the shoes. Indent each shoe at the top with the bone tool, and bend the tips upwards (Figure 3). To make the head, roll 1 oz (28 g) of skin color modeling paste into an egg shape. Gently pinch in the middle to form a nose, and press in the wide end of a decorating tip to mark the mouth. Use a toothpick to mark eyes and nostrils. Roll two tiny balls of skin color modeling paste for ears, and indent with the bone tool. Roll tiny sausages of black modeling paste for the hair. To form the turban, roll ¼ oz (7 g) of white modeling paste into a ball. Indent with your thumb and make a shallow diagonal cut at the front. Roll a tiny piece of yellow modeling paste into a teardrop. Flatten and mark lines to form a feather. Roll out the rest of the yellow modeling paste and cut an arc-shaped collar (Figure 4).

3. To assemble the figure, bend the pants at the knees and orient the waist so that the figure leans backwards. Insert a piece of dry spaghetti into the middle of the pants, leaving enough extending from the top to provide support through to the head. Press on the belt and shirt, and affix the shirt front decorations. Press the collar and head onto the spaghetti. Affix the ears, place the turban on top of the head, and secure the feather

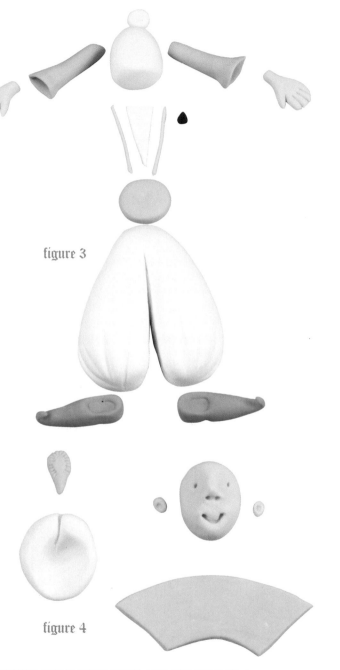

figure 3

figure 4

at the top of the turban. Affix the hair and paint on facial features with the gel food color. Insert toothpicks that extend horizontally at the shoulders and press on the sleeves and hands. Set aside to dry for six hours.

The buildings

4. Roll out 7 oz (198 g) of light brown modeling paste and cut using the template on page 123. To make the turrets, roll ¾ oz (21 g) of sand color modeling paste into a rounded cylinder, and cut out a wedge so that it fits onto the cake corner. Mark three windows using the wide end of a decorating tip and hollow out with the sharp knife. Affix a thin sausage of dark brown modeling paste under each window. To make the turret roof, role ¾ oz (21 g) of dark brown modeling paste into a ball. Shape the ball into a teardrop, and cut out a wedge so that it fits onto the cake corner (Figure 5). Repeat to make three more turrets and roofs. Set aside to dry for three hours.

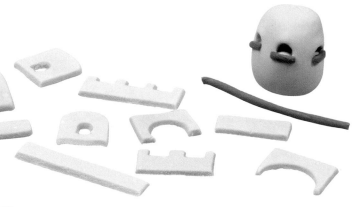

figure 5

Cake and cake board

5. Thinly roll out the green rolled fondant and cover the cake board. Trim the edges and set aside to dry for three hours. Level the cake with the serrated knife and turn it upside down onto a flat surface. Spread buttercream generously on the top and sides. Roll out the turquoise rolled fondant, wrap the cake, and trim the edges with the pizza cutter. Transfer to the cake board and position in the middle. Affix the carpet base in the middle of the cake and lay the carpet on top.

Tilt it forward slightly and affix with royal icing. Thickly roll out the white rolled fondant and cut six flowers with the flower cutter. Re-roll gently to distort the flowers into cloud shapes, and affix on top of the cake. Affix the buildings along the sides of the cake and affix a turret and turret roof at each corner. Roll the remaining dark brown and sand color modeling paste into small sausages. Place one sausage at the base of every turret, and intersperse the rest between the buildings. Affix Aladdin in the middle of the carpet and set aside to dry for three hours.

Remove all non-edible supports
before serving the cake.

Goldilocks and the Three Bears

 **mischievous girl named Goldilocks came upon a house belonging to a family of bears.** The bears were out for a walk, and Goldilocks let herself into the house. She saw three bowls of porridge and sampled each one. After eating all of the porridge in the smallest bowl, Goldilocks proceeded to the living room. There, she saw three chairs. She sat on all of them, eventually breaking the smallest chair. Then Goldilocks headed for the bedroom. She lay on all three beds, and fell asleep on the smallest one. Goldilocks was still sleeping when the bears returned from their walk. They saw the damage she had done and found her sleeping in the bedroom. Goldilocks woke up, saw the three bears, and ran away.

Materials

3 lb 1¼ oz (1.4 kg) modeling paste (page 12), divided and tinted to make:

    3½ oz (100 g) dark brown

    4 oz (100 g) white

    1 oz (28 g) light blue

    1 oz (28 g) skin color

    1 oz (28 g) yellow

    2 oz (57 g) purple

    2 oz (57 g) pink

    3½ oz (100 g) sand color

    1 lb 12 oz (794 g) brown

    ¼ oz (7 g) black

    2 oz (57 g) green

    1 oz (28 g) dark blue

1 batch royal icing (page 13), tinted brown

Brown and red gel food color

9 x 3-inch (23 x 7.6 cm) round cake (pages 9-10)

1 batch buttercream (page 11)

2 lb 14 oz (1.3 kg) rolled fondant (page 12), divided and tinted to make:

    2 lb (900 g) white

    3½ oz (100 g) orange

    10½ oz (300 g) pink

12-inch (30.5 cm) round cake board

Tools

Rolling pin

Small sharp knife

Marking tool

Decorating bag and tip

Pieces of sponge

Toothpicks

Bone tool

Dry spaghetti

Fine paintbrush

Pizza cutter

Serrated knife

7-inch (17.8 cm) cake round or large plate

The bed

1. Roll out 3 oz (85 g) of dark brown modeling paste and cut the bed frame using the template on page 124. Roll 2½ oz (71 g) of white modeling paste into a thick rectangle for the mattress. Roll ½ oz (14 g) of white modeling paste into a smaller rectangle for the pillow and marking creases with the marking tool (Figure 1). Set aside to dry for three hours. Assemble the bed with royal icing. Support with pieces of sponge and set aside to dry for six hours.

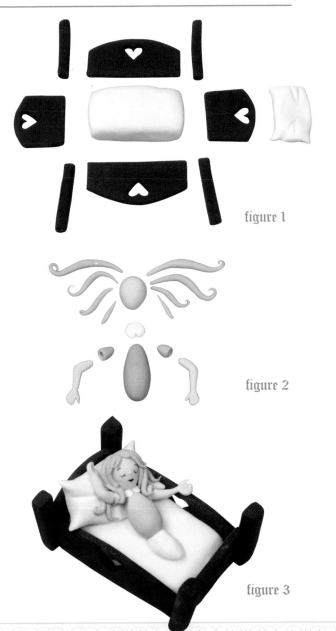

figure 1

Goldilocks

Start building this figure after the bed is dry, as it is assembled directly onto the bed.

2. Form the dress by rolling ⅔ oz (20 g) of light blue modeling paste into an elongated egg shape. Roll the remaining light blue modeling paste into two small cones for sleeves, and indent at the wide end with the bone tool. Divide the skin color modeling paste in half. Roll one half into an egg shape for the head and add a tiny ball for the nose. Roll the other half into two cylinders for the arms. Bend at the elbows and flatten at one end to form hands. Cut with the sharp knife to separate the thumb, and make shallow cuts to form fingers. Roll a little white modeling paste into a ball, flatten, and make a small cut at the front to form a collar. Roll the yellow modeling paste into several long sausages for hair (Figure 2).

figure 2

figure 3

3. Position the dress so that it reclines on the pillow. Place a small lump of white modeling paste below the dress, for legs. (This area will be covered by the blanket, so the color doesn't really matter.) Affix the sleeves and arms on either side of the dress and affix the collar and head at the top. Paint on facial features with the gel food color and affix the hair (Figure 3). Set aside to dry for three hours.

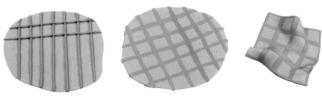

figure 4

The blanket

4. Thinly roll out the purple modeling paste. Roll ½ oz (14 g) of pink modeling paste into several very thin sausages and lay them on the purple modeling paste in a crisscross pattern. Roll with a rolling pin just until integrated. Cut into a 3 x 3-inch (7.6 x 7.6 cm) square and gently crumple (Figure 4). Arrange over Goldilocks, taking care to cover up her legs, and set aside to dry for three hours.

figure 5

The bears

5. Start with the baby bear, and follow the same steps to build the mama and papa bear, only in larger proportions. To make the snout, roll ½ oz (14 g) of sand color modeling paste into a ball, then shape into a rounded cone. Make a cut across the top of the cone, and down the sides. Make a perpendicular cut upwards from the top of the cone, and affix a small triangle of dark brown modeling paste for the nose (Figure 5). Make the head by rolling 1 oz (28 g) of brown modeling paste into a ball. Double-check the proportion of the head and the snout and adjust as necessary. Mark eyes with a toothpick and roll two small balls of brown modeling paste for the ears. Indent each ear with the bone tool. Roll two tiny sausages of dark brown modeling paste for the

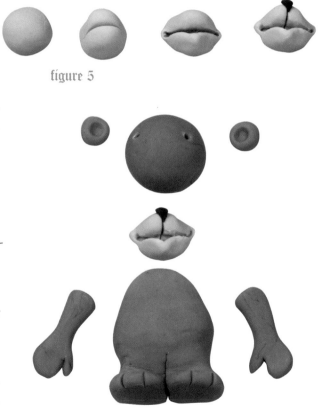

figure 6

eyebrows. To make the body, roll 1½ oz (42 g) of brown modeling paste into an egg shape. At the wider end of the egg, press in a bit on either side to shape legs, and flatten out the feet. Use the marking tool to mark a line down the middle of the legs, and mark paws. Divide ½ oz (14 g) of brown modeling paste in half and shape two cylinders for the arms. Flatten at one end to make paws, and make a small cut to separate the thumb. Roll a small ball of brown modeling paste for the tail (Figure 6).

6. To assemble the bear, insert a piece of dry spaghetti into the body, leaving enough extending from the top to provide support through to the head. Press the head onto the spaghetti and affix the snout and ears. Roll small balls of white and black modeling paste for the eyes, and affix at the spots marked with the toothpick and affix the eyebrows. Insert a toothpick to support the arm that extends outwards, and affix the arms. Add creases for elbows using the marking tool. You'll affix the tail on the smallest bear after he is dressed, but the tails on the mama and papa bear can be affixed now, too.

7. To make the bears' clothing, thinly roll out the green, dark blue, and remaining pink modeling paste, and cut using the templates on page 125. Frill the bottom of the apron by rolling a toothpick over the bottom edge (Figure 7). Affix the green overalls on the baby bear, then detail lines and dots with a toothpick. Press on the buttons with the bone tool, mark a separation between the legs using the back of a knife, and attach the tail. Affix the dark blue tie on the papa bear, and the pink apron on the mama bear. Set aside to dry for three hours.

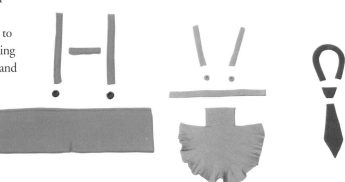

figure 7

Cake and cake board

8. Level the cake with the serrated knife and turn it upside down onto a flat surface. Spread buttercream generously on the top and sides. Roll out the white rolled fondant, wrap the cake, and trim the edges with the pizza cutter. Use your thumb and forefinger to pinch an even trim along the top edge of the cake. Transfer to the cake board and position in the middle. Thinly roll out the orange rolled fondant. Cut with the cake round and affix on top of the cake. Roll 7 oz (198 g) of pink rolled fondant into a thick 29-inch (73.6 cm) sausage and wrap around the bottom of the cake. Roll the remaining pink rolled fondant into a thin 22-inch (55.9 cm) sausage and wrap around the orange circle at the top of the cake. Affix the bed and bears on the cake with royal icing and set aside to dry for three hours.

Remove all non-edible supports before serving the cake.

Cinderella

inderella's mother died when she was young, and her father was remarried to a rather mean woman who had two very lazy daughters. Cinderella was responsible for all the chores, while the others did nothing around the house. Cinderella wore rags, while the others wore fine clothes. One night, the prince held a ball for all the young women in the kingdom. Cinderella couldn't attend because of her chores and wept sadly. Suddenly, her fairy godmother appeared. She transformed a pumpkin into a coach, some mice into horses, and Cinderella's rags into a magnificent gown. "Go to the ball," said the kindly woman, "but be home by midnight!" Cinderella enchanted everyone at the ball—including the prince. At the stroke of midnight, she ran from the palace, accidentally leaving a glass slipper behind. The prince searched far and wide to find the girl whose foot fit the slipper. Of course, only Cinderella's foot fit perfectly. The two fell in love, were married, and lived happily ever after.

Materials

1 lb 14¾ oz (870 g) modeling paste (page 12), divided and tinted to make:

    10½ oz (300 g) orange

    5 oz (142 g) forest green

    4½ oz (127 g) dark gray

    1¼ oz (42 g) light gray

    2 oz (57 g) skin color

    1 oz (28 g) yellow

    1½ oz (42 g) white

    2 oz (57 g) dark brown

    2 oz (57 g) light brown

    1 oz (28 g) turquoise

1 teaspoon (5 ml) CMC

Blue, brown, and red gel food color

9 x 3-inch (23 x 7.6 cm) round cake (pages 9-10)

1 batch buttercream (page 11)

2 lb 10½ oz (1.2 kg) rolled fondant (page 12), divided and tinted to make:

    2 lb (900 g) white

    10½ oz (300 g) sand color

12-inch (30.5 cm) round cake board

1 batch royal icing (page 13)

Tools

Bone tool

Small sharp knife

Marking tool

Rolling pin

Large leaf cutter

Leaf veiner

Empty egg cartons

Plastic straws

Sharp scissors

Dry spaghetti

Fine paintbrush

Toothpicks

Pizza cutter

Serrated knife

Textured rolling pin

7-inch (17.8 cm) cake round or large plate

Decorating bag and tip

Instructions

The pumpkin

1. Shape the orange modeling paste into a large ball and flatten gently at the top and bottom. Press in at the top with the bone tool, and mark thick lines with the marking tool that extend from the top to the bottom. Mark thinner lines between the thick lines using the sharp knife. Roll ⅛ oz (4 g) of forest green modeling paste into a cylinder. Bend to form a stem, and mark a few lines for texture (Figure 1). Affix the stem to the pumpkin and set aside to dry for three hours.

figure 1

figure 2

Leaves and tendrils

2. Add the CMC to the remaining forest green modeling paste to make it particularly stiff. Thinly roll out ⅛ oz (4 g) and cut a leaf using the leaf cutter. Lay the leaf on the leaf veiner and press gently to indent (Figure 2). Repeat to make a total of 20 leaves, arranging them in egg cartons so that they are slightly bent. Set aside to dry for three hours. Roll ⅛ oz (4 g) of forest green modeling paste into a thin sausage. Twist the sausage around a straw to form a tendril (see page 51). Repeat to make a total of 19 tendrils. (This will give you a few spare tendrils, as they tend to break easily.) Carefully remove the tendrils from the straws, and set aside to dry for six hours.

figure 3

Cinderella

3. To make the dress, roll 3 oz (85 g) of dark gray modeling paste into a ball. Shape the ball into a cone and make it narrower about three-quarters of the way up from the bottom to form a waist. Gently press down at the top to form a neckline,

and press in the sides to form grooves for the arms. Widen the bottom by pressing in with your fingers and shaping the hem (Figure 3). Roll 1 oz (28 g) of light gray modeling paste into two tapered cylinders for sleeves. Widen the cuff of each sleeve with the bone tool and bend gently at the elbows. Thinly roll out the remaining ¼ oz (7 g) of light gray modeling paste and cut into a triangle for the handkerchief. Roll 1 oz (28 g) of skin color modeling paste into an egg shape for the head. Add a tiny ball of skin color modeling paste for the nose and mark eyes with a toothpick. To make the hands, roll two small teardrops of skin color modeling paste. Flatten the wider ends, cut with the sharp knife to separate the thumb, and make shallow cuts to form fingers. To make the feet, roll two small sausages of skin color modeling paste and bend at the ankles. Shape a little skin color modeling paste into a teardrop for the neck and flatten. Roll the yellow modeling paste into several long sausages for the hair. Make a small rectangular piece for the bangs, and mark vertical lines with the marking tool. Roll out a little dark brown modeling paste and cut two small squares for patches to the dress. Mark several stitches on each patch with the sharp knife (Figure 4). Thinly roll out the white modeling paste and cut out the apron using the template on page 126. Gently crimp together the top of the apron to form creases, and fold one of the strips to form a ribbon (Figure 5).

4. Assemble the figure on a flat surface. Fold the dress at the knees so that the figure

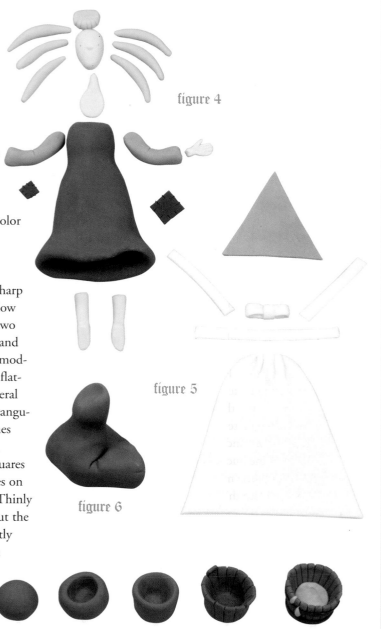

figure 4

figure 5

figure 6

figure 7

46

is kneeling (Figure 6). Insert a piece of dry spaghetti into the neckline, leaving enough extending from the top to provide support through to the head. Press the neck and head onto the spaghetti. Paint on facial features with the gel food color, and affix the hair and handkerchief. Affix a patch on the skirt, then affix the apron around the waist. Arrange the skirt of the apron so that it lays flat on your work surface, and affix the ribbon and straps at the back of the figure. Affix the other patch on a sleeve, then affix the sleeves and hands, arranging them so that they rest on Cinderella's lap. Affix the feet at the back of the figure and set aside to dry for six hours.

The bucket

5. Roll the light brown modeling paste into a ball. Press your thumb into the top of the ball and push up the sides. Flatten the bottom and mark vertical lines all around, inside and out, with the marking tool. Roll out ¼ oz (7 g) of dark brown modeling paste and cut two strips. Affix the strips around the bucket. Roll out the turquoise modeling paste. Press some of it in the bottom of the bucket, and shape a few drops for affixing around the bucket (Figure 7). Shape the remaining turquoise modeling paste into a small puddle. (You'll place this under the bucket when arranging it on the cake.) Form a dishrag by thinly rolling out ¼ oz (7 g) of sand color rolled fondant, and drape it over the edge of the bucket.

The mice

6. To form the body, roll 1¼ oz (35 g) of dark gray modeling paste into a teardrop and flatten the bottom. Use the remaining ¼ oz (7 g) of dark gray modeling paste to roll two tiny balls, for ears, and one thin sausage, for the tail. Flatten the balls and press on either side of the teardrop, near the pointed end. Twist the sausage gently and affix at the rounded end. Mark eyes and a mouth using a toothpick, and affix a tiny ball of sand color rolled fondant for the nose. Mark a curve with the marking tool for the legs. Follow the same technique with the remaining dark brown modeling paste to make a second mouse.

Cake and cake board

7. Level the cake with the serrated knife and turn it upside down onto a flat surface. Spread buttercream generously on the top and sides. Roll out the white rolled fondant, wrap the cake, and trim the edges with the pizza cutter. Use your thumb and forefinger to pinch an even trim along the top edge of the cake. Transfer to the cake board and position in the middle. Thinly roll out 3½ oz (100 g) of sand color rolled fondant. Roll once using the textured rolling pin, cut out a circle using the cake round, and affix on top of the cake. Roll the remaining sand color rolled fondant into a 29-inch (73.6 cm) sausage and wrap around the bottom of the cake. Affix the pumpkin, Cinderella, the mice, and the bucket on the cake. (Don't forget to place a small puddle of turquoise modeling paste under the bucket.) Affix one of the tendrils to the top of the pumpkin with a little royal icing, and arrange the rest of the tendrils and leaves on the cake and cake board. Set aside to dry for three hours.

Remove all non-edible supports before serving the cake.

Jack and the Beanstalk

ack was a good-hearted, sometimes thoughtless boy who lived with his poor widowed mother. When the family ran out of money, Jack was sent to market to sell the family cow. He returned home not with a handful of money, but magic beans, which his mother promptly threw out the window in disgust. The seeds grew into a giant beanstalk overnight, and in the morning, Jack climbed the beanstalk. He found a terrible giant and gold coins at the top. Jack escaped with a handful of coins, which he and his mother used for food and other essentials. When the coins were spent, Jack climbed the beanstalk again. This time, he found the giant and a hen that laid golden eggs. Jack grabbed the hen and ran down the beanstalk. The giant was in hot pursuit, but Jack reached the ground first and cut down the beanstalk. With an unlimited supply of golden eggs, Jack and his mother never had to worry about money again, and they lived happily ever after.

Materials

2 teaspoons (10 ml) CMC

5 lb 6 oz (2.4 kg) modeling paste (page 12),
divided and tinted to make:

    1 lb (454 g) forest green

    4 lb (1.8 kg) brown

    1 oz (28 g) blue

    1½ oz (42 g) orange

    1 oz (28 g) red

    1 oz (28 g) yellow

    1½ oz (42 g) skin color

9 x 3-inch (23 x 7.6 cm) round cake (pages 9-10)

1 batch buttercream (page 11)

2 lb (900 g) white rolled fondant (page 12)

14 x 14-inch (35.6 x 35.6 cm) cake board

Light blue gel food color

1 batch royal icing (page 13), tinted brown

Tools

Rolling pin

Large leaf cutter

Small leaf cutter

Leaf veiner

30 pieces of floral wire,
each 2 inches (5 cm) in length

Fine paintbrush

Plastic straws

Pizza cutter

Serrated knife

Pieces of sponge

Marking tool

Toothpicks

Decorating bag and tip

Bone tool

Dry spaghetti

Instructions

Leaves and tendrils

1. Add the CMC to the forest green modeling paste to make it particularly stiff. Thinly roll out ⅛ oz (4 g) and cut a leaf using the small leaf cutter. Lay the leaf on the leaf veiner and press gently to indent (Figure 1). Use 7 oz (198 g) of the modeling paste to make 32 small leaves and 18 large leaves. Lay a piece of floral wire on the bottom of a leaf, on the veined side. Fold the leaf over the wire and press the sides together. Repeat to fold wires in 15 large leaves and 15 small leaves. Pinch the rest of the leaves together at the bottom without adding any wire (Figure 2). Set aside to dry for six hours. Roll ⅛ oz (4 g) of forest green modeling paste into a thin sausage. Twist the sausage around a straw to form a tendril (Figure 3). Repeat to make 30 tendrils. (This will give you a few spare tendrils, as they tend to break easily.) Carefully remove the tendrils from the straws, and set aside to dry for six hours.

The beanstalk

2. Roll 3 lb 6 oz (1.6 kg) of brown modeling paste into a large cone. Make roots by drawing the bottom of the cone outwards in several directions, forming several thick sausages with tapered ends. You want the roots to extend beyond the edge of the cake, so make sure they are quite long. Draw the top of the cone upwards so that it is long and tapered, and twist (Figure 4).

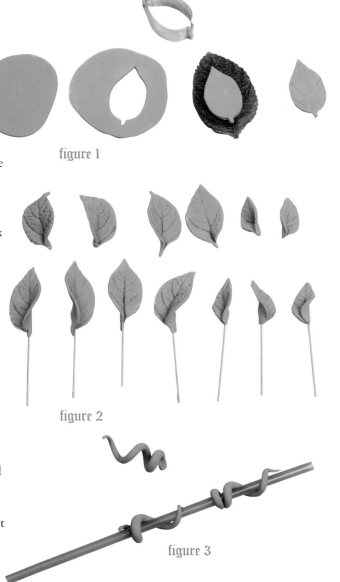

figure 1

figure 2

figure 3

Cake and cake board

3. Level the cake with the serrated knife and turn it upside down onto a flat surface. Spread buttercream generously on the top and sides. Roll out the white rolled fondant, wrap the cake, and trim the edges with the pizza cutter. Transfer to the cake board and position in the middle. Position the beanstalk on the center of the cake, and arrange the stalk and roots so that the weight is evenly dispersed. Use the remaining brown modeling paste to form extra roots, arranging them in places where more support is needed. Use pieces of sponge to support the beanstalk as it dries. Supporting the beanstalk can be quite difficult, so be sure to incorporate plenty of roots and use several pieces of sponge for support. Set aside to dry for 24 hours.

Jack

Start building this figure after the beanstalk is dry, as it is assembled directly onto the beanstalk.

4. To form the pants, roll the blue modeling paste into a 5-inch (12.7 cm) sausage. Fold the sausage in half and bend at the knees. Add creases using the marking tool. To make the shirt, roll 1 oz (28 g) of orange modeling paste into a cone. Mark a line down the middle with the marking tool, and press in at the bottom, shaping the edge to form flaps. Roll a small ball of orange modeling paste for the collar and flatten. Roll the rest of the orange modeling paste into two elongated cones for the sleeves. Indent the sleeves at the wider end with the bone tool and add creases at the elbows with the marking tool. Roll out ¼ oz (7 g) of yellow rolled fondant and cut a

figure 4

narrow strip for the belt. To make the buckle, roll a tiny ball of red modeling paste, flatten, and indent with the bone tool. Roll the rest of the red modeling paste into two identical teardrops for the shoes. Flatten each shoe along the bottom and bend near the rounded end to form the heel. To make the hands, roll two small teardrops of skin color modeling paste. Flatten the wider ends, cut with the sharp knife to separate the

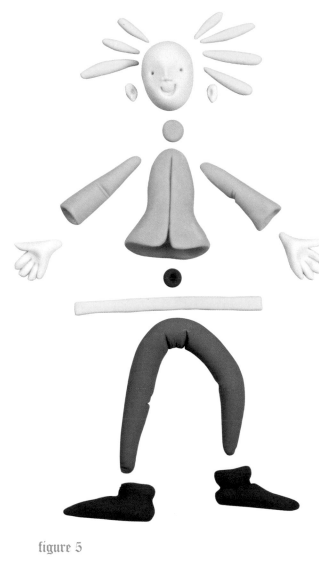

figure 5

thumb, and make shallow cuts to form fingers. Roll two tiny balls of skin color modeling paste for the ears and indent with the bone tool. Roll the remaining skin color modeling paste into an egg shape for the head. Gently pinch a nose, and use a toothpick to mark eyes and nostrils. Mark a mouth by pressing in the wide end of a decorating tip. Roll several short sausages of yellow modeling paste for the hair (Figure 5).

5. Assemble Jack directly onto the beanstalk. Begin with the legs, arranging them so that they straddle one of the roots. Insert a piece of dry spaghetti into the top of the pants, leaving enough extending from the top to provide support through to the head. Affix the shoes to the bottom of the pants and support with pieces of sponge until dry. Wrap the belt around the shirt and affix the buckle at the front. Press the shirt and collar onto the spaghetti, position the shirt so that it leans backwards onto the beanstalk. Insert toothpicks horizontally into the top of the shirt and press on the sleeves and hands. Affix the hair around the back of the head, then press onto the spaghetti. Paint on eyes with the gel food color.

Finishing touches

6. Insert the large leaves with the floral wire along the length of the beanstalk. Insert the smaller leaves with the floral wire along the base of the cake. Affix the tendrils and remaining leaves on the cake and cake board with a little royal icing. Set aside to dry for three hours.

Remove all non-edible supports before serving the cake.

The Pied Piper

**he village of Hamelin was overrun with rats.** The villagers tried everything to get rid of them, but their efforts were to no avail. Eventually, the mayor promised a generous reward to anyone who could rid the village of its rats. A stranger with a pipe arrived to take up the challenge. He piped a tune and wandered through the town, attracting all of the rats. He continued to play as he walked out of the town, leading the rats away. The townspeople were delighted to be rid of the rats, but the mayor refused to pay the promised reward. The next day, the stranger returned with his pipe. He piped another tune—one that attracted the village children. And this time he led them out of the town.

Materials

2 lb 14¾ oz (1.3 kg) modeling paste (page 12), divided and tinted to make:

- 13 oz (368 g) gray
- ¾ oz (21 g) dark brown
- 1 oz (28 g) orange
- 3 oz (85 g) red
- 1 oz (28 g) yellow
- 1 oz (28 g) light purple
- 1 oz (28 g) skin color
- 3½ oz (100 g) sand color
- 8½ oz (240 g) light brown
- 12 oz (339 g) dark green

Brown food color marker

6 lb 4 oz (2.8 kg) rolled fondant (page 12), divided and tinted to make:

- 1 lb 6 oz (623 g) light brown
- 5 oz (140 g) light blue
- 9 oz (255 g) white
- 4 lb (1.8 kg) light green

1 batch royal icing (page 13)

9 x 13 x 3-inch (23 x 33 x 7.6 cm) rectangle cake (pages 9-10)

14 x 14-inch (36 x 36 cm) square cake board

1 batch buttercream (page 11)

Tools

Bone tool

Toothpicks

Marking tool

Rolling pin

Small flower cutter

Small sharp knife

Fine paintbrush

Wooden skewer

Pieces of sponge

Decorating bag and tip

Pizza cutter

Serrated knife

Rubber spatula

Mice

1. To make the body, shape ⅓ oz (9 g) of gray modeling paste into an elongated teardrop. Roll two small balls of gray modeling paste for the ears. Indent both ears with the bone tool and affix near the pointed end of the body. Use a toothpick to mark eyes just in front of the ears. Roll a tiny bit of gray modeling paste into a tapered sausage for the tail, twist a few times, and affix at the rounded end of the body (Figure 1). Repeat to make a total of 36 mice. Set aside to dry for three hours.

Piper

Make the pipe in advance, as it must dry before being affixed to the piper.

2. Make the pipe by rolling ¼ oz (7 g) dark brown modeling paste into a cylinder that widens slightly at one end. Indent several holes along one side using a toothpick, and set aside to dry for two hours. To make the sleeves, roll ⅓ oz (9 g) of orange modeling paste into a thick sausage. Roll an equal amount of red modeling paste into a thinner sausage. Wrap the red sausage around the orange sausage and roll on a flat surface until they merge into a single smooth sausage. Cut in half widthwise to form two sleeves. Shape each sleeve so that it flares at one end. Indent the wider end with the bone tool and bend at the elbow (Figure 2). To make the shirt, roll the yellow modeling paste into a cone. Use the marking tool to mark a seam down the front of the shirt, and shape the corners at the bottom to form

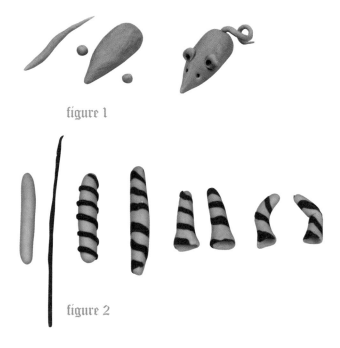

figure 1

figure 2

flaps. To make the collar, roll out a little light purple modeling paste and cut with the flower cutter. Roll a small sausage of light purple modeling paste for the neck and flatten at both ends. To make the shoes, divide the rest of the light purple modeling paste in half and roll each half into an elongated teardrop. Bend at a 90° angle to form ankles, flatten along the bottom, and mark creases with the marking tool. To make the pants, roll the remaining orange modeling paste into a ball. With the knife, make a vertical cut extending from the top of the ball to the bottom and shape either side of the cut into ballooning pant legs. Mark creases with the marking tool and indent the bottom opening of each pant leg with the bone tool. To make the legs, roll 1 oz (28 g) of red modeling paste into a cylinder and cut in half widthwise. Shape the knees and mark creases, leaving one leg slightly straighter than the other. Roll ⅔ oz (19 g) of skin color modeling paste into an egg shape for the head. Mark eyes with a toothpick. With the blunt tip of the paintbrush, mark an open mouth that is wide enough to hold the small end of the pipe. Affix two tiny balls of skin color modeling paste for the ears and a tiny sausage for the nose. Roll tiny balls of dark brown modeling paste for the eyes and the remaining dark brown modeling paste into small sausages for the hair. Roll the remaining skin color modeling paste into a cylinder and cut in half widthwise. Flatten both halves at one end to form hands. With the sharp knife, separate the thumb and make shallow cuts to mark fingers (Figure 3).

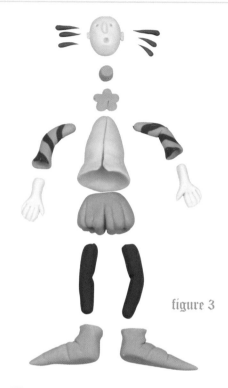

figure 3

3. To assemble the figure, insert a wooden skewer into the straighter leg, leaving enough extending from the top to provide support through to the head. Press on the pants and affix the other leg. Affix the shoes at the bottom of the legs and press the shirt, collar, neck, and head onto the skewer. Affix the hair and eyes, and mark eyebrows using the brown food color marker. Position the pipe in the mouth and affix using a little royal icing. Affix the sleeves and hands to the shirt, orienting them so that they support the pipe. Support the figure with pieces of sponge and set aside to dry for three hours.

Houses and tower

4. Make a house by rolling ⅔ oz (19 g) of sand color modeling paste into a teardrop. Flatten the bottom and sides and pinch along the top to form a base for the roof. Mark a door on the front of the house: for the rounded top, press in the wide end of a decorating tip; for the straight sides, use a sharp knife. To make a roof, roll out ½ oz (14 g) of red modeling paste and cut out a ¾ x 2-inch (2 x 5 cm) rectangle. With the marking tool, mark a line widthwise down the middle, then use the wide end of a decorating tip to press in a shingle pattern (Figure 4). Repeat to make three more houses and roofs. Affix the roofs to the houses and set aside to dry for three hours.

figure 4

To make the tower, roll the remaining sand color modeling paste into a cylinder. Make a roof by flattening a small ball of light brown modeling paste into a disk. Roll ¼ oz (7 g) of light brown modeling paste into a cone. Affix the disk and cone on top of the cylinder and set aside to dry for three hours.

Trees

5. Roll 1 oz (28 g) of light brown modeling paste into a cylinder. Shape the cylinder into a trunk by adding creases and contours with the marking tool and bone tool. To make a treetop, shape 1½ oz (42 g) of dark green modeling paste into a cone. Repeat to make seven more trunks and treetops. Affix the treetops to the trunks and set aside to dry for three hours.

Cake and cake board

6. Thinly roll out 14 oz (396 g) of light brown rolled fondant and cover the cake board. Roll out the light blue rolled fondant and cut a 3 x 14-inch (7.6 x 36 cm) rectangle with a wavy edge along one long side. Lay the light blue rolled fondant along one edge of the cake board. Trim the brown and blue rolled fondant edges with the pizza cutter. Set aside to dry for three hours. Level the cake with the serrated knife and turn it upside down onto a flat surface. Spread buttercream generously on the top and sides with the rubber spatula. Roll 4 oz (113 g) of white rolled fondant into a ball and flatten the bottom. Place on one corner of the cake, forming the base for a hill. Using the remaining 5 oz (142 g) of white rolled fondant, roll 2 smaller balls of varying sizes, flatten their bottoms, and position on top of the cake.

7. Roll out 3 lb 9 oz (1.6 kg) of light green rolled fondant and wrap the cake, taking care to press down the fondant in the valleys between the hills. Trim the edges with the pizza cutter. Carefully transfer the cake to the cake board, positioning it so that it is parallel to the river. Roll the remaining light brown rolled fondant into a 44-inch (113 cm) sausage and affix around the base of the cake. Roll the remaining light green rolled fondant into a long strip and position it so that it winds from between two of the hills on the top of the cake, down around one corner of the cake, and onto the cake board. Affix the houses and steeple in a cluster on the highest hill. Affix the piper on the cake board, at the corner diagonal to the houses, using a little royal icing. Arrange the trees all over the cake and affix the mice so that they make a trail from the town to the piper, winding between the hills and down the green strip to the cake board. Set aside to dry for three hours.

Remove all non-edible supports before serving the cake.

Pinocchio

eppetto was a kindly carpenter with no children. He carved a piece of wood into a puppet and named it Pinocchio. Pinocchio wasn't a real boy, but Geppetto loved him dearly. It wasn't long, however, before Pinocchio started getting into mischief. The Blue Fairy warned him to behave, but Pinocchio ignored her advice. He eventually grew donkey ears and was sold to a circus. As Geppetto searched for his missing boy, he was swept into the sea and swallowed by a whale. Pinocchio was swallowed by the same whale and met Geppetto in its belly. Together they escaped from the whale's belly, but now they were floating at sea. Pinocchio risked his own life to save Geppetto. The Blue Fairy rewarded him for this selfless act by turning him into a real boy.

Materials

1 lb 9½ oz (722 g) modeling paste (page 12), divided and tinted to make:

  8 oz (227 g) light brown

  4 oz (113 g) white

  ¼ oz (7 g) green

  1½ oz (42 g) yellow

  1¾ oz (49 g) black

  6 oz (170 g) blue

  4 oz (113 g) red

Silver luster powder

4 lb 13 oz (2.2 kg) rolled fondant (page 12), divided and tinted to make:

  1 lb 8 oz (680 g) dark brown

  14 oz (397 g) light brown

  2 lb (907 g) white

  7 oz (198 g) green

10 x 10-inch (25 x 25 cm) square cake board

9 x 3-inch (23 x 7.6 cm) round cake (pages 9-10)

1 batch buttercream (page 11)

1 batch royal icing (page 13)

Tools

Toothpicks

Rolling pin

Small sharp knife

Small flower cutter

Bone tool

Wooden skewer

Decorating bag and tip

Pieces of sponge

Fine paintbrush

Vegetable peeler

Pizza cutter

Serrated knife

Rubber spatula

Open-curve crimper

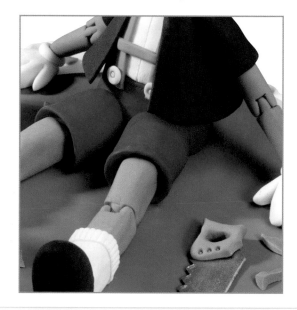

Instructions

Pinocchio

Make the nose in advance, as it must dry before being affixed to the figure.

1. Make the nose by rolling a small sausage of light brown modeling paste. Set aside to dry for two hours. Make the shirt by rolling 2½ oz (71 g) of white modeling paste into a cone. Thinly roll out the green modeling paste and cut three thin strips for suspenders. For the hat, roll 1¼ oz (35 g) of yellow modeling paste into a cone shape and indent at the bottom to accommodate the head. Roll two tiny balls of yellow modeling paste for the buttons and three small balls to make the bow tie. Add detail using toothpicks and the bone tool. To make the collar, roll out a little white modeling paste and cut with the flower cutter. Roll over the flower with the rolling pin to make the collar even thinner. Thinly roll out ½ oz (14 g) of black modeling paste and cut the jacket and hair using the templates on page 126. To make the sleeves, roll ½ oz (14 g) of black modeling paste into two small cones and indent at the wider end with the bone tool. Roll 1½ oz (42 g) of light brown modeling paste into an egg shape for the head. Mark the mouth with the wide end of a decorating tip and indent with a wooden skewer to make a place for the nose. With a toothpick, draw the corners of the mouth upwards at each end, pushing outwards to make the cheeks. Indent the eyes with the toothpick as well. Roll tiny balls of white modeling paste and tinier balls of blue modeling paste for the eyeballs.

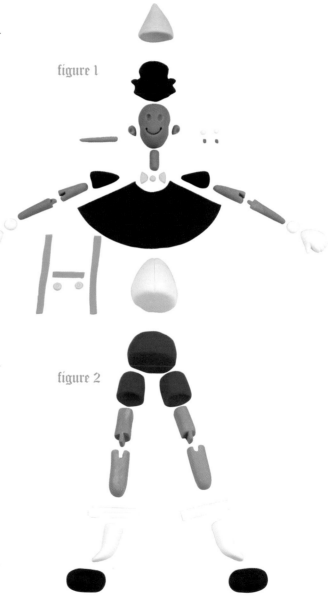

figure 1

figure 2

Roll two tiny elongated teardrops of black modeling paste for the eyebrows. Roll two small balls of light brown modeling paste for the ears and indent with the bone tool. Roll a thin cylinder of light brown modeling paste for the neck. To make the arms, roll 1 oz (28 g) of light brown modeling paste into a thin cylinder. Cut the cylinder in half widthwise, then cut each half into two pieces with a jagged, joint-like cut at the elbow. To make the gloves, divide ½ oz (14 g) of white modeling paste in two, shape into teardrops, and flatten. With a sharp knife, separate the thumb and make shallow cuts to mark fingers. Roll two small balls of white modeling paste and flatten to form glove cuffs (Figure 1). Make the seat of the pants by rolling 2 oz (57 g) of red modeling paste into a sausage and flatten both ends. Roll the remaining 2 oz (57 g) of red modeling paste into a thinner sausage, cut in half widthwise, and flatten all four ends to make the pant legs. Make the legs by rolling 1½ oz (42 g) of light brown modeling paste into a cylinder. Cut the cylinder in half widthwise to make two legs. Cut each leg into two pieces with a jagged, joint-like cut at the knee. To make socks, divide ⅔ oz (21g) of white modeling paste in half and shape each half into a teardrop. Flatten the rounded end and bend the pointed end to one side. To make sock cuffs, roll out two thin strips of white modeling paste and mark vertical lines widthwise with the small sharp knife. To make the shoes, divide ⅔ oz (21 g) of black modeling paste in half and shape each half into a stubby sausage with rounded ends (Figure 2). Assemble the figure on a flat surface. Begin by affixing the pant legs in front of the pants seat, so that they extend forwards. Affix the legs, socks, and shoes, and wrap the sock cuffs around the top of the socks. Insert a wooden skewer into the top of the pants seat, leaving enough extending from the top to provide

support through to the head. Press on the shirt and affix the suspenders and buttons. Wrap the jacket around the back of the shirt and affix the collar on top and the bow tie at the front. Affix the sleeves, arms, glove cuffs, and gloves, and support with pieces of sponge until dry. Press the neck and head onto the skewer. Attach the hair, eyeballs, eyebrows, ears, and hat. Affix the nose in the middle of the face with a little royal icing. Set aside to dry for six hours.

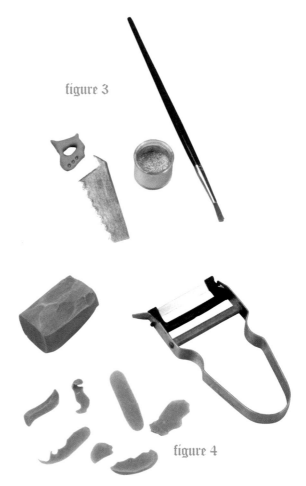

figure 3

figure 4

Saw

2. Shape the remaining yellow modeling paste into a flat square. Form a handle by cutting a hole in the middle and shaping curves and edges. Mark three holes along one side of the handle with a toothpick. Thinly roll out ¼ oz (7 g) of white modeling paste and cut into a blade shape using a sharp knife. Set aside to dry for 30 minutes. Mix the silver luster powder with a little water and paint the blade (Figure 3). Set aside to dry for 30 minutes, then affix the blade to the handle with a little royal icing and set aside to dry for three hours.

Wood and wood shavings

3. Roll the remaining light brown modeling paste into a short sausage and flatten both ends. Shave all around with the vegetable peeler to make an irregular surface (Figure 4). Keep the shavings for decorating the cake.

Cake and cake board

4. Thinly roll out the dark brown rolled fondant and cover the cake board. Trim the edges with the pizza cutter. Roll the light brown rolled fondant into a 40-inch (102.4 cm) sausage and affix around the edge of the cake board. Set aside to dry for three hours. Level the cake with the serrated knife and turn it upside down onto a flat surface. Spread buttercream generously on the top and sides with the rubber spatula. Roll out the white rolled fondant, wrap the cake, and trim the edges with the pizza cutter. Use the open-curve crimper to crimp along the top edge of the cake. Transfer the cake to the cake board and position in the middle. Roll the green rolled fondant into a 29-inch (74 cm) sausage and affix around the base of the cake.

figure 5

Fringed carpet

5. To make a fringe, thinly roll out ½ oz (14 g) of blue modeling paste and cut out an 8½ x 8½-inch (22 x 22 cm) square. Cut deep slits into one side, leaving a wide strip uncut along the opposite edge. Tightly roll up the square along the uncut edge. Gather up and re-roll the scraps of blue modeling paste, cut out a thin rectangular strip, and wrap around the top of the fringe to secure (Figure 5). Repeat to make three more fringes. To make the carpet, thinly roll out the remaining blue modeling paste. Cut a 7 x 7-inch (18 x 18 cm) square and lay on top of the cake, taking care that the corners hang evenly over the edge of the cake. Affix a fringe at each corner of the carpet with a little royal icing and support with pieces of sponge. Set aside to dry for six hours.

Finishing touches

6. Affix Pinocchio, the saw, and the block of wood on the cake with a little royal icing. Scatter wood shavings all around and set aside to dry for three hours.

Remove all non-edible supports
before serving the cake.

The Princess and the Pea

here was once a prince who wanted to marry a genuine princess. He bade farewell to his parents and embarked on a trip around the world in search of such a princess. He met several alleged princesses, but none was real enough for him, and he returned to the palace in a rather grumpy mood. One stormy night, a girl claiming to be a princess knocked on the palace door seeking shelter. The queen decided to test whether she was really a princess. She placed three peas in the girl's bed, covered them with several fluffy mattresses, and bid the princess a pleasant sleep. In the morning, the queen asked the princess how she had slept. "Terribly!" said the girl. "There were lumps in my bed! I must be black and blue all over!" This proved that she was a real princess. She soon married the prince, and they lived happily ever after.

Materials

1 lb 15 oz (878 g) modeling paste (page 12),
divided and tinted to make:

   5 oz (142 g) light orange

   4 oz (113 g) light blue

   4 oz (113 g) light pink

   5 oz (142 g) yellow

   5 oz (142 g) light green

   5 oz (142 g) white

   2 oz (57 g) skin color

   1 oz (28 g) dark brown

Food color markers

Black, brown, and red gel food color

4 lb 9 oz (2.1 kg) rolled fondant (page 12),
divided and tinted to make:

   1 oz (28 g) light pink

   1 lb 15 oz (878 g) pink

   2 lb 7 oz (1.1 kg) white

   1 oz (28 g) light purple

   1 oz (28 g) turquoise

9 x 3-inch (23 x 7.6 cm) round cake
(pages 9-10)

1 batch buttercream (page 11)

11-inch (28 cm) round cake board

1 batch royal icing (page 13)

Tools

Marking tool

Small sharp knife

Toothpick

Fine paintbrush

Rolling pin

Serrated knife

Rubber spatula

Pizza cutter

12-inch (30.5 cm) cake round or plate

Frill cutter

Decorating bag and tip

Mattresses

Make the mattresses in advance, as they must dry before the princess can be assembled onto them.

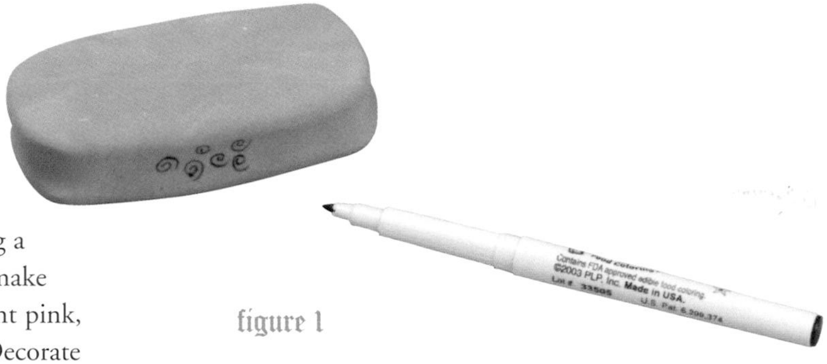

1. Shape 4 oz (113 g) of light orange modeling paste into a thick 2 x 4-inch (5 x 10 cm) rectangle. Press in at the sides with your fingers and decorate using a food color marker (Figure 1). Repeat to make four more mattresses using light blue, light pink, yellow, and light green modeling paste. Decorate with the food color markers or marking tool. Set aside to dry for three hours.

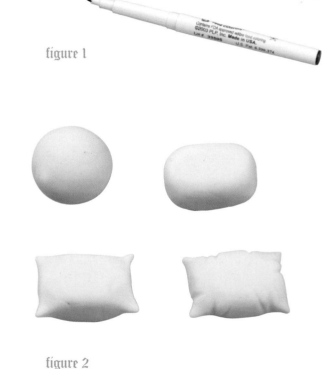

figure 1

Pillows

2. Shape 1 oz (28 g) of yellow modeling paste into a ball and flatten into a thick 1 x 2-inch (2.5 x 5 cm) rectangle. Pinch out at the corners to make a pillow shape. Mark creases with the marking tool (Figure 2). Repeat to make five more pillows: two using white modeling paste and two using light green and orange modeling paste. Make each pillow a little different by altering the dimensions. Set aside to dry for three hours.

Princess

3. To make the nightgown, roll 3 oz (85 g) of white modeling paste into a ball. Shape the ball into a cone and narrow it about three-quarters of the way up from the bottom to form a waist. Gently press the point in and flatten to form a neckline. Widen the bottom by flattening it outwards and

figure 2

shape the hem by pressing in at the bottom with your thumb. Form two gentle bumps in the skirt for the legs (Figure 3). Make the neck by shaping a little skin color modeling paste into a teardrop. Flatten the wide end so that it fits into the neckline of the nightgown. Make the head by rolling ⅔ oz (19 g) of skin color modeling paste into an egg shape. Roll a tiny ball of skin color modeling paste for the nose and affix to the head. Roll several sausages of dark brown modeling paste for the hair. To make the arms, divide ½ oz (14 g) of skin color modeling paste in half and shape each half into a sausage. Bend gently at the elbows and flatten at one end to make hands. With the sharp knife, separate the thumb and make shallow cuts to mark fingers. To make the legs, divide the remaining skin color modeling paste in half and shape each half into a small sausage. Point at one end to form toes and bend at the ankles (Figure 4).

4. Assemble the figure directly onto one of the mattresses. Position the nightgown first, arranging it so that the princess lies at an angle. Insert a toothpick into the neckline, leaving just enough extending from the top to support the neck and head. Press on the neck and head and affix the hair. Paint on facial features with the gel food color. To make the blanket, thinly roll out 1 oz (28 g) of light pink rolled fondant and cut into a 3 x 5-inch (7.6 x 12.8 cm) rectangle. Arrange the blanket on top of the princess, creating folds and waves. Affix the arms on top of the blanket and the feet sticking out of the nightgown at the bottom. Set aside to dry for three hours.

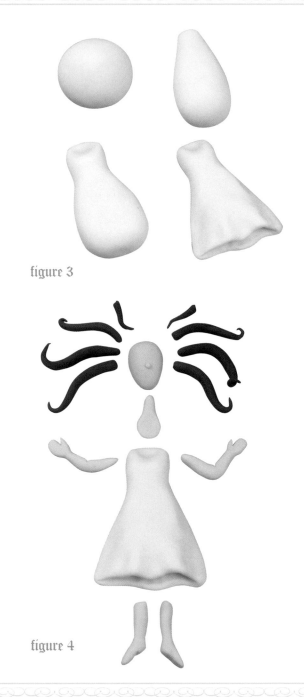

figure 3

figure 4

Cake and cake board

5. Level the cake with the serrated knife and turn it upside down onto a flat surface. Spread buttercream generously on the top and sides with the rubber spatula. Roll out 2 lb (907 g) of white rolled fondant and wrap the cake, trimming the edges with the pizza cutter. Transfer to the cake board and position in the middle. Roll out 1 lb 12 oz (793 g) of pink rolled fondant, place the cake round in the center, and cut around it with the frill cutter. Carefully position the pink rolled fondant on top of the cake so that an even edge hangs all around. Roll the remaining white rolled fondant into a 25-inch (64 cm) sausage and affix around the base of the cake. Roll the remaining pink rolled fondant into a thinner sausage of the same length and affix just above the white sausage.

6. Lay a mattress on the cake, a little off to one side. Use royal icing to affix another mattress on top, orienting it so that it is slightly askew. Make a blanket by thinly rolling out the light purple rolled fondant. Cut into a 2 x 4-inch (5 x 10 cm) rectangle and lay on the mattress, making sure that some of the blanket hangs over the sides. Affix another mattress onto the blanket, then make another blanket using the turquoise rolled fondant and lay that on top. Place the fourth mattress on top, then affix to it the mattress with the princess. Affix the pillows on top of the cake and set aside to dry for three hours.

Remove all non-edible supports before serving the cake.

Puss in Boots

miller's youngest son inherited a cat from his father's humble estate. The cat promised the son great riches in return for a sack and a pair of boots. The son obliged, and the cat began implementing his plan. First, he caught prey and gave it to the king as a gift from his master, the 'Marquis of Carabas.' Of course, the Marquis of Carabas was just a pseudonym for the miller's son. The cat then convinced the king to provide the Marquis with a fine suit of clothes. When the king's daughter saw the Marquis dressed in king's clothes, she fell in love. The miller's son soon married the princess, and the cat lived out the rest of its life in well-earned luxury.

Materials

1 tsp (5 ml) CMC

3 lb ¼ oz (1.4 kg) modeling paste (page 12), divided and tinted to make:

    2 lb (907 g) light brown

    8½ oz (241 g) gray

    ½ oz (14 g) yellow

    3 oz (85 g) red

    1 oz (28 g) white

    3¼ oz (91 g) dark brown

9 x 3-inch (23 x 7.6 cm) round cake (pages 9-10)

1 batch buttercream (page 11)

2 lb 9 oz (1.2 kg) rolled fondant (page 12), divided and tinted to make:

    2 lb (907 g) white

    9 oz (255 g) green

12-inch (30.5 cm) round cake board

1 batch royal icing (page 13)

Tools

Rolling pin

Pizza cutter

Frill cutter

Marking tool

Toothpicks

9-inch (23 cm) round cake pan

Small sharp knife

Fine paintbrush

Decorating bag and tip

Bone tool

Small round cutter

Pieces of sponge

Dry spaghetti

Serrated knife

Rubber spatula

7-inch (17.8 cm) cake round or plate

Instructions

Fence

Make this a day in advance, as the pieces must dry for 12 hours.

1. To make the fence on top of the cake, add the CMC to 8 oz (227 g) of light brown modeling paste. Thickly roll out and cut a 6 x 2½-inch (15 x 6.5 cm) rectangle and cut with the pizza cutter to make three rectangles, one measuring 2⅓ x 2½ inches (6 x 6.5 cm) and the other two measuring each 1½ x 2½ inches (4 x 6.5 cm). Use the frill cutter to cut one long side of each rectangle, forming the top of the fence posts. Mark vertical lines with the marking tool to separate planks of wood and use a toothpick to mark nails at the top and bottom of each plank. Press the fence along the inside rim of a round cake pan (the one you used to bake the cake is perfect), so that the smooth side of the modeling paste is flush against the pan. Set aside to dry for 12 hours.

Puss in Boots

2. Shape the head by rolling 1½ oz (42 g) of gray modeling paste into a ball. Stretch the bottom four-fifths of the ball horizontally and press down gently on the sides to flatten. With the sharp knife, make a few small cuts on each flattened side for whiskers. Mark a smiling mouth using the wide end of a decorating tip and pull upward with a toothpick to mark slanted eye sockets. Cut a small line upwards in the middle of the mouth and create a half-circle just below it by

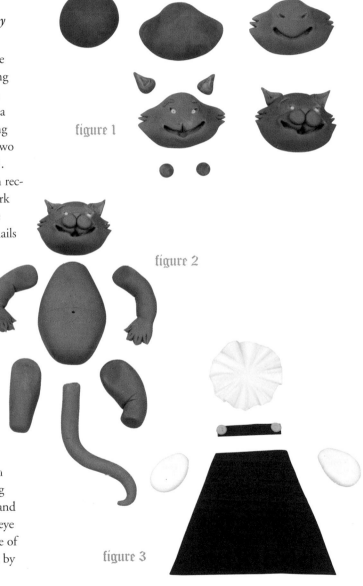

figure 1

figure 2

figure 3

pressing in with the blunt tip of the fine paint-brush. Press tiny balls of yellow modeling paste into each eye socket. Add tiny sausages of gray modeling paste for eyebrows. To make the ears, shape two small teardrops of gray modeling paste and two smaller teardrops of light brown modeling paste. Press the light brown teardrops onto the gray teardrops using the bone tool and affix at the top of the head. To make cheeks, roll two tiny balls of gray modeling paste, flatten into disks, and affix above the mouth. Affix a small triangle of light brown modeling paste for the nose (Figure 1).

To make the body, roll 3 oz (85 g) of gray modeling paste into an egg shape. Flatten the wider end at the back bottom, so that the piece is able to stand alone when Puss is placed in a sitting position. Press two flat areas near the front bottom for affixing the legs and two near the top for the arms, creating a gentle diamond shape. Mark a belly button in the middle with a toothpick. To make legs, roll 1½ oz (42 g) of gray modeling paste into a thick sausage and cut in half widthwise. Shape each half so that it tapers slightly at one end and bend one leg slightly at the knee. To make each arm, roll ¾ oz (21 g) of gray modeling paste into a cylinder. Bend gently at the elbow and wrist,, and mark creases with the back of a knife. Flatten the area below the wrist to form paws, and make a few small cuts with the sharp knife for claws.

To make the tail, roll ¾ oz (21 g) of gray modeling paste into a long sausage that tapers at one end and twist gently at the thinner end (Figure 2). To make the cape, thinly roll out 1¼ oz (35 g) of red modeling paste and cut according to the template on page 127. Roll two small balls of yellow modeling paste for the buttons and indent each button with the bone tool. To make the collar, thinly roll out

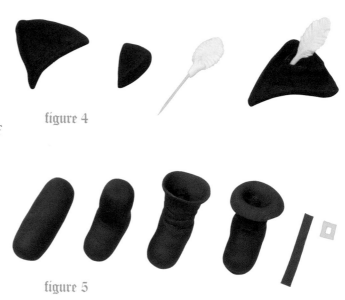

figure 4

figure 5

some white modeling paste, cut with the small round cutter. and frill the edges by rolling with a toothpick. To make the sleeves, divide ¼ oz (7 g) of white modeling paste in half and shape each half into a thick egg-shaped disk (Figure 3). Make the hat by shaping 1¼ oz (35 g) of red modeling paste into a thick triangle. Pinch the corners of the triangle together to form sharp points and draw the edges of the hat upwards. Roll ½ oz (14 g) of red modeling paste into a smaller triangle, pinch its corners and draw up its edges, and affix on top of the larger triangle. Roll a small amount of white modeling paste into a teardrop and flatten the wider end. Use the sharp knife to make small cuts all around the flattened portion, forming a feather. Press one end of a toothpick into the narrow end of the feather and insert the other end of the tooth-pick into the top triangle of the hat (Figure 4).

To make a boot, roll 1½ oz (42 g) of dark brown

modeling paste into a thick sausage and bend in the middle at a 90° angle. Mark creases on the inside of the bend using the marking tool. Flatten the bottom to form the sole and press in at the top to form an opening. Press the edges of the opening to thin them and pull them outward and down to form a wide, floppy cuff. Thinly roll out a little dark brown modeling paste and cut a thin strap. Roll out a little yellow modeling paste and cut a square buckle (Figure 5). Wrap the strap around the boot and affix the yellow buckle at the front. Repeat to make a second boot and set both aside to dry for three hours.

3. Assemble the figure on a flat surface and against a support, such as a box or pan placed on a table or countertop. Begin by affixing the tail at the back, then affix the cape so that it wraps around the body. Position the body so that its back leans against the support. Affix the strap and buttons at the front top corners of the cape. Affix the straight leg so that it extends forward and affix a boot at the bottom. Arrange the bent leg so that the knee is raised, affix the boot at the bottom, and place pieces of sponge beneath the knee for support. Affix the sleeves and arms on either side of the body, positioning one of the arms so that it rests on the bent knee and the other arm with the paw on the ground. Insert a piece of dry spaghetti into the top of the body and press on the collar and head. Set aside to dry for six hours.

Cake and cake board

4. Level the cake with the serrated knife and turn it upside down onto a flat surface. Spread butter-cream generously on the top and sides with the rubber spatula. Roll out the white rolled fondant and wrap the cake, trimming the edges with the pizza cutter. Transfer to the cake board and position in the middle. To make the fence around the cake, thickly roll out the remaining light brown modeling paste and cut a 20 x 2½-inch (50 x 6.5 cm) rectangle. Cut with the pizza cutter to make six ½ x 2½-inch (1.3 x 6.5 cm) rectangles, one 1½ x 2½-inch (3.8 x 6.5 cm) rectangle, five 2 x 2½-inch (5 x 6.5 cm) rectangles, one 2½ x 2½-inch (3.8 x 6.5 cm) rectangle, and one 3 x 2½-inch (7.6 x 6.5 cm) rectangle. Use the frill cutter to cut along one long side of each large rectangle, one side of each square, and one short side of each small rectangle, forming the top of the fence posts. Mark vertical lines with the marking tool to separate planks of wood and use a toothpick to mark nails at the top and bottom of each plank. Affix the fence all around the cake with the marked side facing outward and with some of the single planks positioned at an angle. Roll out the green rolled fondant, place the cake round in the center, and trace around it with the pizza cutter to cut out a circle. Affix on top of the cake. Carefully remove the dried fence from the rim of the cake pan and affix on top of the cake using royal icing, such that the marked side of the fence faces the cake's center. Lean the posts very slightly inward toward the center of the cake and support with pieces of sponge until dry. Position Puss in Boots with his back against the fence and affix the hat on the straight knee. Set aside to dry for three hours.

*Remove all non-edible supports
before serving the cake.*

Rapunzel

 **here was a girl named Rapunzel who was stolen by a witch and locked in a tower.** She grew to be a beautiful girl, with a lovely voice and magnificent hair. Every day, the witch would call "Rapunzel, Rapunzel, let down your hair!" and the girl would hang her long braids out the window so that the witch could climb up. One day, a prince heard Rapunzel singing and was enchanted. He watched the witch's ritual and imitated it, climbing up Rapunzel's locks. The prince and Rapunzel soon fell in love, but when the witch discovered their secret, she cut Rapunzel's hair and sent her to a faraway land. The witch tricked the prince into climbing the tower again. When he realized Rapunzel was gone, he fell from the window and was blinded by thorns. The lovers were separated for years, but when they were finally reunited, Rapunzel's tears of joy fell into the prince's eyes and restored his sight.

Materials

2 tsp (10 ml) CMC

5 lb 11⅔ oz (2.6 kg) modeling paste (page 12), divided and tinted to make:

    4 lb 3½ oz (1.9 kg) gray

    6½ oz (184 g) brown

    7 oz (198 g) green

    3 oz (85 g) light gray

    1⅔ oz (47 g) skin color

    6 oz (179 g) yellow

9 x 9 x 3-inch (23 x 23 x 7.6 cm) square cake (pages 9-10)

1 batch buttercream (page 11)

2 lb (907 g) white rolled fondant (page 12)

12 x 12-inch (30.5 x 30.5 cm) square cake board

1 batch royal icing, tinted gray (page 13)

Blue gel food color

Tools

Rolling pin

Pizza cutter

Brick-textured rolling pin

Small rectangle cutter

Small sharp knife

Empty wine bottle

Wooden skewers

Pieces of sponge

Sharp scissors

Piece of cardboard

Cellophane tape

Serrated knife

Rubber spatula

Decorating bag and tip

Toothpick

Fine paintbrush

Wire cutters

Instructions

Walls

1. To make a wall, add ½ tsp (2.5 ml) of CMC to 8 oz (227 g) of gray modeling paste to make it particularly stiff. Thickly roll out and cut a 3 x 8-inch (7.6 x 20.5 cm) rectangle using the pizza cutter. Roll horizontally with the brick-textured rolling pin to imprint a brick pattern. Use the small rectangle cutter to cut out evenly spaced sections along one long side of the rectangle, forming the top of the wall (Figure 1). Repeat to make two more walls. Cut one of the walls in half to make two walls measuring 3 x 4 inches (7.6 x 10.2 cm). Set aside to dry for six hours.

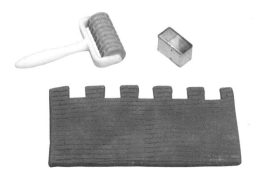

figure 1

Tower

Make this piece in advance, as Rapunzel is assembled directly into the dried tower.

2. Add the remaining 1½ tsp (7.5 ml) of CMC to 1 lb 8 oz (681 g) of gray modeling paste and thickly roll out. Cut an 8 x 11-inch (20.5 x 28 cm) rectangle with the pizza cutter and roll horizontally with the brick-textured rolling pin to imprint a brick pattern. Use the small rectangle cutter to cut out eight evenly spaced sections along one long side of the rectangle, forming the top of the tower. Use a wooden skewer to pierce eight evenly spaced holes along the top, one below each section cut out with the rectangle cutter. Cut out a 2 x 2-inch (5 x 5 cm) window in the middle of the rectangle, near the top, then round the top of the window with the sharp knife. Wrap the rectangle around the empty wine

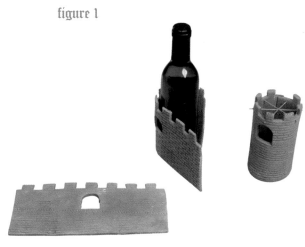

figure 2

bottle, textured side facing outward, and trim the edge where the two sides join to form a smooth seam (Figure 2). Roll out ½ oz (14 g) of gray modeling paste and cut six small strips. Affix the strips horizontally over the seam to secure. Support with pieces of sponge and set aside to dry for 24 hours.

Roof

3. Make a base upon which to dry the roof by cutting the cardboard according to the template on page 128. Roll up to form a cone and place on the tower to make sure it fits. (The exact size of your roof will depend on the bottle you used to shape the tower.) Trim the cone until it fits the tower. Roll out 3 oz (85 g) of brown modeling paste, place the cardboard base on top, and cut out along the base's lines using the sharp knife. Seal the cardboard base's seam with cellophane tape, then lay the modeling paste over the cardboard cone. Join the edges to form a smooth seam (Figure 3). Set aside to dry for 24 hours.

figure 3

Cake and cake board

4. Level the cake with the serrated knife and turn it upside down onto a flat surface. Spread buttercream generously on the top and sides with the rubber spatula. Roll out the white rolled fondant and wrap the cake, trimming the edges with the pizza cutter. Transfer to the cake board and position in the middle. Position the tower first, placing it about 2 inches (5 cm) from one corner of the cake, with the seam of the tower facing that corner. Affix the shorter walls first, arranging them on either side of the tower at a 90° angle, with the textured sides facing outward.

Generously apply royal icing between the tower and the walls to secure and support with pieces of sponge. Affix the longer walls next, positioning them at 90° angles to the shorter walls to form a square courtyard, and ensuring that their textured sides also face outward. Generously apply royal icing at the corners and support with pieces of sponge. Set aside to dry for six hours.

Vines and rocks

5. To make a vine, roll ½ oz (14 g) of green modeling paste into a sausage that tapers at one end. Affix the wider end of the sausage at the base of the cake and draw the tapered end upwards towards the castle. Affix smaller tapered sausages to the main sausage, orienting them in various directions. Use the rest of the green modeling paste to make nine more vines of various sizes and lengths. Make some extra long so that they creep up the walls as well. Affix all vines around the cake. Set aside a little light gray modeling paste for making the tip of the roof. Use the rest, as well as 3 oz (85 g) each of the brown and gray

figure 4

modeling paste, to make 45 rocks of various sizes and shapes (Figure 4). Affix around the base of the cake, filling in the spaces between the vines.

Rapunzel

6. Roll ⅔ oz (19 g) of skin color modeling paste into an egg shape for the head. Roll a small ball of skin color modeling paste for the nose and mark eyes with a toothpick. Mark the mouth by pressing in the wide end of a decorating tip. Make the neck by shaping ⅔ oz (19 g) of skin color modeling paste into a teardrop. Insert a skewer firmly through the teardrop, leaving just enough extending from the top to support the head and leaving the rest extending from the bottom. (This end of the skewer must be long enough to be inserted securely into the cake while still keeping the head level with the win-

figure 5

dow of the tower.) To make the hand, roll a little skin color modeling paste into a teardrop and flatten. With the sharp knife, separate the thumb and make shallow cuts to mark fingers. Make some of the hair by rolling 1 oz (28 g) of yellow modeling paste into several sausages that taper at both ends (Figure 5).

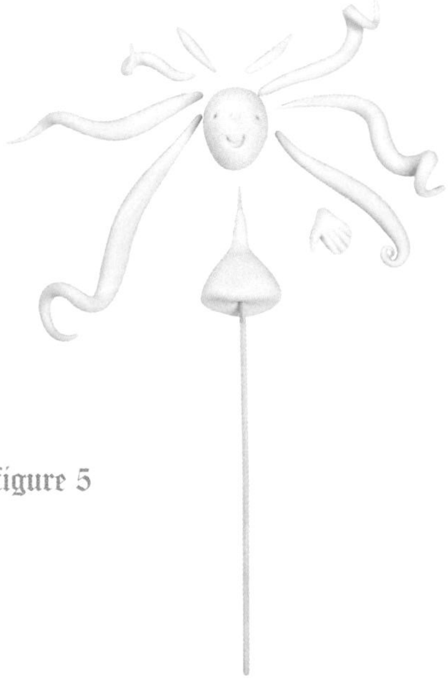

7. To assemble the figure, press the head onto the portion of the skewer extending from the top of the neck. Paint on eyes with the gel food color and affix the hair around the head. Carefully bring the skewer inside the tower and position it so that the face appears at the window. Insert the skewer firmly into the cake. Affix the hand near one corner of the window and draw some long pieces of hair out the other side of the window. Roll the remaining yellow modeling paste into tapered sausages of varying lengths and thicknesses. Affix these along the tower, arranging them so that they twirl and interweave as they cascade down onto the cake.

Finishing touches

8. Insert wooden skewers in the holes at the top of the tower so that they form a support for the roof. Trim the ends of the skewers using the wire cutters. Roll six small balls with the remaining brown modeling paste and press one ball over the end of each skewer. Place the roof on the tower, allowing it to rest on the skewers. Form a small cone of gray modeling paste and affix on top of the roof.

Remove all non-edible supports
before serving the cake.

The Snow Queen

 **little girl named Gerda and a little boy named Kay were the very best of friends.** One day, the Snow Queen gave Kay two kisses: a piece of ice fell into his eye and a grain of frozen sand landed in his heart. Under her spell, his heart grew ever colder. He soon abandoned his friendship with Gerda, going with the Snow Queen to her castle of ice. In the spring, Gerda went on an adventurous voyage to find Kay. When she finally found him, she wept with relief. Her warm tears melted Kay's frozen heart, and they left the frozen palace together hand in hand.

Materials

9-inch (23 cm) cone cake (pages 9-10)

1 batch buttercream (page 11)

2 lb (907 g) white rolled fondant (page 12)

11-inch (28 cm) round cake board

1 lb 8¼ oz (687 g) modeling paste (page 12),
divided and tinted to make:

    1 lb 5 oz (595 g) white

    2½ oz (57 g) skin color

    ¾ oz (21 g) light blue

Pinch of CMC

Silver and blue luster powder

1 batch royal icing (page 13)

Brown, pink, and blue gel food color

Tools

Serrated knife

Rubber spatula

Pizza cutter

Rolling pin

Small silicone face mold

Toothpick

Small sharp knife

Bone tool

Dry spaghetti

Pieces of sponge

Plastic cling wrap

Fine paintbrush

Decorating bag and tip

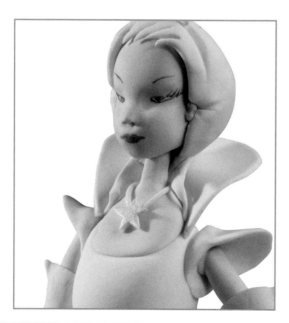

Instructions

Cake

1. Level the cake with the serrated knife and place on a flat surface. Spread buttercream generously on all sides with the rubber spatula. Roll out the white rolled fondant and wrap the cake, trimming the edges with the pizza cutter. Transfer to the cake board and position in the middle.

Silver crown and necklace

2. Thinly roll out a little white modeling paste and cut a jagged crown and a small star for the pendant. Roll a tiny sausage of white modeling paste for the chain. Set aside to dry for 30 minutes. Mix a little silver luster powder with water and paint the crown and necklace. Set aside to dry for three hours.

Snow Queen

3. To make the bodice, roll 2 oz (57 g) of white modeling paste into an egg shape. Narrow near the smaller end to form the waist and flatten the bottom. Press down the top of the wider end to form the neckline and press in at the sides just below the neckline to form grooves for the arms (Figure 1). Roll 1½ oz (42 g) of skin color modeling paste into an elongated ball, press into the silicone face mold, and carefully remove (Figure 2). Use a toothpick to enhance the nostrils and shape other facial features as desired. Shape tiny ears using a little skin color modeling paste. Roll the light blue modeling paste into a ball. Press in with your thumb to form a bowl shape for the hair and shape the sides so that it fits around the ears. Use

figure 1

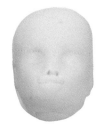

figure 2

the sharp knife to make a few cuts at the front for bangs. Make the neck by shaping ⅔ oz (19 g) of skin color modeling paste into a cone. Mold the wide end of the cone so that it fits into the neckline of the bodice. Divide the remaining skin color modeling paste in half and form two small cylinders for the upper arms. To make a glove, roll ½ oz (14 g) of white modeling paste into a sausage, gently pinch in to form the elbow and wrist and flatten the area below the wrist to make the hand. Use the sharp knife to separate the thumb and make shallow cuts to mark fingers. Indent the top of the glove (where it will be attached to the arm) using the bone tool and flare the edges outward with your fingers. Repeat to make a second glove. Use ¼ oz (7 g) of white modeling paste to make two triangular sleeves for affixing at the top of the arms. Form the collar by adding a pinch of CMC to ¼ oz (7 g) of white modeling paste. Roll out and cut according to the template on page 127 (Figure 3).

4. To assemble the figure, insert a piece of dry spaghetti into the middle of the cake, leaving enough extending from the top to provide support through to the Snow Queen's head. Press the bodice onto the spaghetti and affix the sleeves, arms, and gloves in the desired position. Support with pieces of sponge. Press the neck onto the spaghetti and affix the silver star necklace with a little royal icing. Press on the head and paint facial features with the gel food color. Affix the hair, crown, and collar, and set aside to dry for six hours.

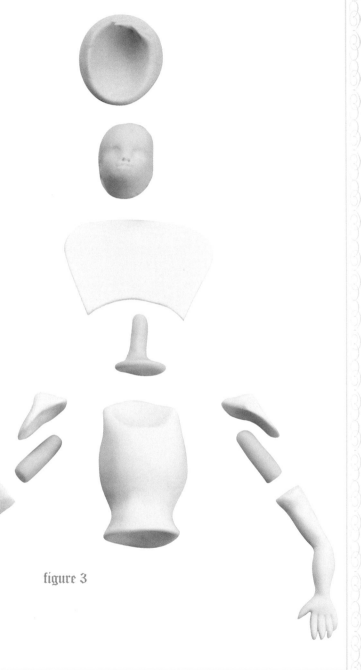

figure 3

figure 4

Skírt

5. Very thinly roll out the remaining white modeling paste. Cut out 40 icicles using the templates on page 127. (Thinly rolled modeling paste dries very quickly, so keep it covered with plastic cling wrap as you work.) Mix a little blue luster powder with water and lightly paint the jagged edges of 20 icicles (Figure 4). Remove the pointed end of two blue-tipped icicles and affix these around the waist of the figure, at the edge of the bodice. Affix the rest of the blue-tipped icicles in a ring around the bottom of the cake by placing a dab of royal icing at the top of each one. Position them so that they overlap slightly and so that the painted edges gently bend onto the cake board. Affix the all-white icicles so that their top points are about 2 inches (5 cm) above the top points of the blue-tipped icicles, positioning them so that they also overlap slightly. Set aside to dry for three hours.

Remove all non-edible supports before serving the cake.

Little Red Riding Hood

ittle Red Riding Hood was a lovely young girl known to all for the bright red cape she wore. One morning, she set off for her granny's house with a basket of treats. "Don't dawdle," warned her mother, "and don't talk to strangers!" Little Red Riding Hood ignored her mother's advice. After picking flowers in the woods, she told a sly wolf where she was going. The wolf arrived at the granny's house before Little Red Riding Hood. He hid the granny in the closet and disguised himself in one of her nightgowns. When Little Red Riding Hood arrived, she mistook the wolf for her granny, but wondered about her unusually large eyes, ears, and teeth. The wolf was just about to gobble her up when a kindly woodsman came by and saved Little Red Riding Hood and her granny.

Materials

3 lb 8¾ oz (1.6 kg) modeling paste (page 12),
divided and tinted to make:

- 1 lb 5 oz (595 g) brown
- 9 oz (255 g) green
- 1½ oz (42 g) pink
- 1½ oz (42 g) orange
- 1½ oz (42 g) purple
- 2 oz (57 g) yellow
- 2 oz (57 g) light blue
- 2½ oz (71 g) white
- 2 oz (57 g) red
- 1½ oz (42 g) skin color
- 1 oz (28 g) sand color
- 7½ oz (212 g) dark gray
- 3½ oz (100 g) light gray
- ¼ oz (7 g) black

Black and red gel food color

4 lb 1 oz (1.8 kg) rolled fondant (page 12),
divided and tinted to make:

- 2 lb 1 oz (935 g) green
- 2 lb (907 g) white

12-inch (30.5 cm) round cake board

9 x 3-inch (23 x 7.6 cm) round cake
(pages 9-10)

1 batch buttercream (page 11)

1 batch royal icing (page 13)

Tools

Small sharp knife

Bone tool

Wooden skewers

Wire cutters

Rolling pin

Small flower cutter

Pieces of sponge

Marking tool

Toothpicks

Fine paintbrush

Pizza cutter

Serrated knife

Rubber spatula

Open-curve crimper

Decorating bag and tip

Instructions

Trees

Build the trees in advance, as the wolf is assembled directly onto a dried tree.

1. To make a tall tree, roll 9 oz (255 g) of brown modeling paste into a ball, then pull the ball into a long cone. Shape the cone into a trunk by marking creases with the sharp knife and making holes with the bone tool. Shape several branches by drawing portions at the top of the trunk upwards and out in various directions. Insert a piece of wooden skewer into each branch, leaving enough extending from the top to support 1 or 2 leaf clumps. To make a leaf clump, roll 1 oz (28 g) of green modeling paste into a lumpy shape (Figure 1). Repeat to make several more leaf clumps of varying shapes and sizes. To assemble the tree, press the leaf clumps onto the skewers. Trim any excess skewer visible above the top leaf clump with wire cutters. Repeat to make another tall tree that is about the same size as the first tree. Make a third tree that is considerably smaller using 3 oz (85 g) of brown modeling paste for the trunk and affixing just one leaf clump. Set aside to dry for three hours.

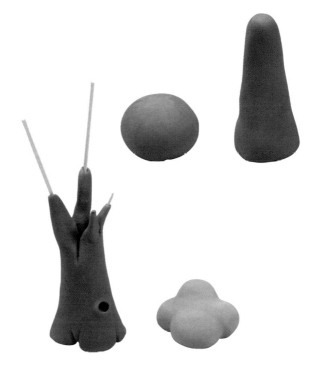

figure 1

Flowers

2. Very thinly roll out ⅛ oz (4 g) of pink modeling paste and cut a flower using the flower cutter. Lay the flower on a piece of sponge and press in the middle with the bone tool to push up the petals. Repeat using 1½ oz (42 g) each of pink, orange, purple, and yellow modeling paste, making a total of 48 flowers. Set aside to dry for three hours.

Little Red Riding Hood

3. To make the dress, roll 1¾ oz (49 g) of light blue modeling paste into a rounded cone. Press in the top to form a neckline, and form a waist by narrowing the cone about three-quarters of the way up from the bottom. Shape the hemline by pressing the bottom of the cone deeply inwards with your thumb and drawing the edges out and downwards with your other fingers (Figure 2).

To form the sleeves, divide the remaining light blue modeling paste in half. Roll each half into a small ball and indent with the bone tool. Make legs by rolling 1½ oz (42 g) of white modeling paste into a cylinder that tapers slightly at one end. Flatten the cylinder slightly and mark a line down the middle with the marking tool. At the narrower end of the cylinder, make a cut with the sharp knife to divide the two legs. Divide ¼ oz (7 g) of white modeling paste in half and roll each half into a small egg shape. Indent with the bone tool to form feet. To make shoes, divide ½ oz (14 g) of red modeling paste in half and roll each half into an egg shape. Use the bone tool to press in the top of each shoe nearer to one end of the egg than the other, making room for the feet. Roll tiny strips of red modeling paste to form the shoe straps. Roll out ½ oz (14 g) of white modeling paste and cut a semi-circle for the apron. Roll a thin sausage of white modeling paste for the collar on the dress. Form the neck by shaping ⅓ (9 g) of skin color modeling paste into a teardrop. Flatten the wide end so that it fits into the neckline of the dress. Make the head by rolling ⅔ oz (19 g) of skin color modeling paste into an egg shape. Roll a tiny ball of skin color modeling paste for the nose and mark eyes using a toothpick. To make the arms, divide ½ oz (14 g) of skin color modeling paste in half and shape each half into sausages. Bend gently to form elbows and flatten at one end to make hands. With the sharp knife, separate the thumb and make shallow cuts to mark fingers. Divide ½ oz (14 g) of yellow modeling paste into three equal pieces, shape each piece into an egg shape, and flatten. Mark bangs on one piece by pressing in vertical lines with the back of a knife

figure 2

figure 3

figure 4

94

(Figure 3). To make the cape, set aside a small ball of red modeling paste (for the wolf's tongue) and roll out the rest. Cut according to the template on page 129 (Figure 4).

4. Insert a wooden skewer into one of the legs, leaving enough extending from the top to provide support through to the head and enough extending from the bottom to reach through foot and shoe firmly into the cake. Press a foot and shoe onto the bottom of the skewer and affix the other foot and shoe on the other leg. Affix the red straps over both feet. Press the dress and neck onto the skewer and affix the apron and collar. Affix the sleeves and arms, arranging the arms so that the hands rest on the apron. Press on the head, affix the hair, and paint on facial features with the gel food color. Wrap the cape around the figure, place the hood on the head, and affix the strap. Support with pieces of sponge and set aside to dry for six hours.

Basket and napkin

5. Pinch off a little sand color modeling paste (for the basket handle) and roll the rest into a ball. Press into a rounded rectangular shape, then press in at the top to create a container. Press horizontal lines all around the outside using the back of the sharp knife. With the sand color modeling paste you set aside, roll a long, thin sausage and flatten to create a strip for the handle (Figure 5). To make the napkin, roll out a little white modeling paste and cut into a rectangle that is slightly larger than the top of the basket. Place the napkin on top of the basket, then affix the handle over the middle of the basket. Set aside to dry for three hours.

figure 5

Wolf

6. Make a front leg by rolling ½ oz (14 g) of dark gray modeling paste into a sausage. Add ¼ oz (7 oz) of light gray modeling paste onto the end of the sausage and roll a few times on a flat surface to create a smooth, seamless join. Flatten the light gray area of the sausage into a paw and make small cuts with the sharp knife to separate the claws (Figure 6). Repeat to make a second front leg. To make the hind legs, roll 1 oz (28 g) of dark gray modeling paste into a cylinder and cut in half widthwise. Bend each half to form a horseshoe shape. To make the paws, divide ¼ oz (7 g) of dark gray modeling paste in half and roll each half into an egg shape. Flatten and make small cuts with the sharp knife to separate claws.

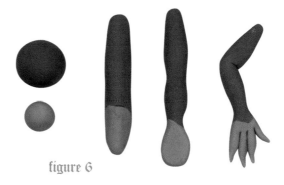

figure 6

Affix to the bottom of the hind legs. To make the body, roll 5 oz (141 g) of dark gray modeling paste into a large teardrop. Flatten at the thick end so that the piece will be able to stand alone when the wolf is placed in a crouching position. Press in either side at the flattened end to make room for the hind legs. To make the face, roll 2 oz (57 g) of light gray modeling paste into a peanut shape. Make a long, shallow cut for the mouth, beginning at the narrow point of the peanut on one side and stretching all the way around one tip to the other side of the narrow point. At the cut tip, make another small cut upwards, perpendicular to the long cut. Widen the mouth using the small sharp knife and your fingers. With a toothpick, mark a few whisker dots above the mouth on either side of the short cut. Roll a little black modeling paste into a ball and affix above the mouth for the nose. Roll the red modeling paste you set aside previously into a long oval shape for the tongue. Make two tiny, sharp cones of white modeling paste for the fangs. Thinly roll out a little black modeling paste and cut into a triangle with a rounded bottom for the fur at the top of the head. Roll tiny balls of yellow modeling paste for the eyes and poke in the middles with a toothpick. Roll tiny strips of dark gray modeling paste for the eyebrows. For the ears, divide ¼ oz (7 g) of dark gray modeling paste in half and roll each half into an elongated diamond shape. Cut off one point of each ear to make a straight edge. For the inside of the ears, roll smaller elongated diamonds of light gray modeling paste and cut off a point to make a straight edge. To make the tail, roll the remaining light gray modeling paste into several sausages with tapered ends (Figure 7).

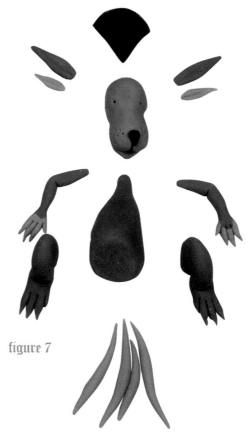

figure 7

7. To assemble the wolf, insert a wooden skewer through the middle of the body, leaving enough extending from the top to provide support through to the head. Affix the hind legs to the sides of the body. Affix the front legs, arranging them so that they wrap around one of the tall dried trees. Press the head onto the skewer and affix the tongue, fangs, and eyes. At the top of the head, affix the patch of black fur, the eyebrows, and the ears. Affix the tail at the back and set aside to dry for six hours.

Cake and cake board

8. Thinly roll out 1 lb 8 oz (680 g) of green rolled fondant and cover the cake board. Trim the edges with the pizza cutter and set aside to dry for three hours. Level the cake with the serrated knife and turn it upside down onto a flat surface. Spread buttercream generously on the top and sides with the rubber spatula. Roll out the white rolled fondant and wrap the cake, trimming the edges with the pizza cutter. Use the open-curve crimper to crimp along the top edge of the cake. Transfer to the cake board, leaving enough room on one side of the board for the smallest tree. Roll 7 oz (198 g) of green rolled fondant into a 29-inch (74 cm) sausage and affix around the base of the cake. Thickly roll out 2 oz (57 g) of green rolled fondant and make plots of grass by cutting out two jagged-edged areas, one a little bigger than the other, with the sharp knife. Affix the plots of grass on top of the cake. Use royal icing to affix the tall trees, wolf, basket, and Little Red Riding Hood to the top of the cake. Affix the little tree on the cake board. Make blades of grass by shaping the remaining 1 oz (28 g) of green modeling paste into several small teardrops. Flatten the bottom of each teardrop and bend the top. Affix flowers and blades of grass scattered about the plots of grass on top of the cake, and affix flowers on the cake board as well. Set aside to dry for six hours.

Remove all non-edible supports
before serving the cake.

Rumpelstiltskin

 **poor miller told the king that his daughter could spin straw into gold.** The king put the girl to the test, ordering her to spin a room full of straw into gold by morning. A little man appeared in the night and spun the straw into gold in exchange for the girl's necklace. The delighted king ordered the girl to spin even more gold the next night. This time, the little man helped out in exchange for the girl's ring. The king was overjoyed. He promised to marry the girl if she could repeat the task again. That night, the little man agreed to spin the gold in exchange for the girl's first-born child. She agreed. The king made the miller's daughter his queen, and a child was soon born. The little man came to collect his debt, but agreed to release the queen from her promise if she could discover his name within three days. The queen guessed the name Rumpelstiltskin just in time, and the little man ran off in a fury, never to be seen again.

Materials

1 tsp (5 ml) CMC

3 lb 11½ oz (1.7 kg) modeling paste (page 12), divided and tinted to make:

    1 lb 12½ oz (807 g) light gray

    1 oz (28 g) orange

    2¼ oz (64 g) skin color

    ¼ oz (7 g) dark brown

    4½ oz (127 g) green

    ½ oz (14 g) light purple

    3 oz (85 g) blue

    ½ oz (14 g) red

    12 oz (340 g) yellow

    3½ oz (100 g) dark gray

    3½ oz (100 g) black

Gold luster powder

9 x 3-inch (23 x 7.6 cm) round cake (pages 9-10)

1 batch buttercream (page 11)

2 lb (907 g) white rolled fondant (page 12)

12-inch (30.5 cm) round cake board

1 batch royal icing (page 13)

Tools

Rolling pin

Pizza cutter

Brick-textured rolling pin

Small sharp knife

9-inch (23 cm) round cake pan

Toothpicks

Bone tool

Marking tool

Wooden skewers
Fine paintbrush

Serrated knife

Rubber spatula

Pieces of sponge

Instructions

The wall

Make this a day in advance, as the pieces must dry for 12 hours.

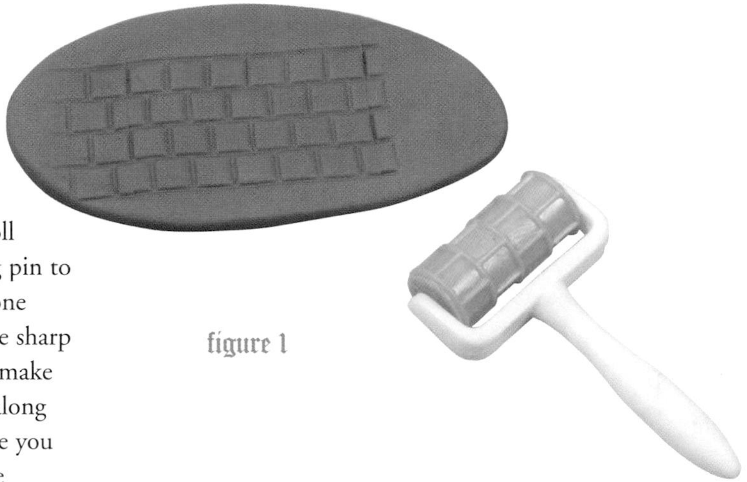

1. Add the CMC to 6 oz (170 g) of gray modeling paste and thickly roll out. Cut with the pizza cutter into a rectangle measuring 12 x 3 inches (30 x 7.6 cm). Roll horizontally with the brick-textured rolling pin to imprint a brick pattern (Figure 1). Along one long edge, follow the brick pattern with the sharp knife, cutting out bricks here and there to make an uneven top for the wall. Press the wall along the inside rim of a round cake pan (the one you used to bake the cake is perfect) so that the smooth side of the modeling paste is flush against the pan (Figure 2). Set aside to dry for 12 hours.

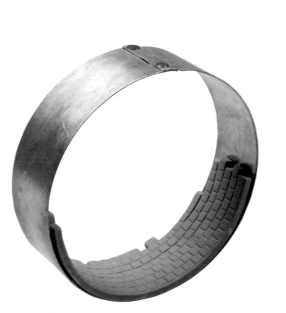

figure 1

Rumpelstiltskin

2. Set aside a tiny ball of orange modeling paste (for the belt buckle) and roll the rest into a long sausage with one end tapered to a point, for the hat. Flatten the round end of the sausage and draw out its edges to form a wide rim, then push up in the middle with your thumb to make a dent for the head. Bend the pointed tip and use the small sharp knife to add a few creases (Figure 3). To make the face, roll 2 oz (57 g) of skin color modeling paste into a rounded triangle shape. Pinch a nose in the upper middle of the face and make wide nostrils with a toothpick. Cut a horizontal line for the mouth, deepen the cut with the sharp knife, and draw upwards at either end

figure 2

with a toothpick to form a wide smile. Mark eyes with a toothpick. Shape pointy ears by rolling two small teardrops of skin color modeling paste and indenting with the bone tool. Roll tiny sausages of dark brown modeling paste for the eyebrows, two small balls for the eyes, and a long thin strip for the hair (Figure 4). Prepare the shirt by rolling 3 oz (85 g) of green modeling paste into a ball. Narrow the ball about one-third of the way up from the bottom to form the waist and pull the area below the waist down into a stump. With your thumb, press the bottom of the stump up and in to form an opening, and with your other fingers pull the edges down and out until they flare. Mark a seam down the front of the shirt using the marking tool and separate the corners at the bottom to form distinct flaps (Figure 5). To make the sleeves, divide the remaining green modeling paste in half and shape each half into a cone that flares at one end. Add creases with the marking tool. To make the collar, roll ¼ oz (7 g) of light purple modeling paste into a ball and flatten into a disk. With the sharp knife, make several tiny cuts around the edge and pull the jagged points outward. Roll the remaining light purple modeling paste into two small balls and flatten for cuffs. To make the hands, roll two small teardrops of skin color modeling paste and flatten. With the sharp knife, separate the thumbs and make shallow cuts to mark fingers. Roll out a little blue modeling paste and cut three small straps for the shirt. Roll the rest of the blue modeling paste into a long cylinder that tapers a little at both ends. Fold the cylinder in half to make the pants and mark creases with the marking tool. To make a shoe, roll ¼ oz (7 g) of red modeling paste into a teardrop. Press in just above

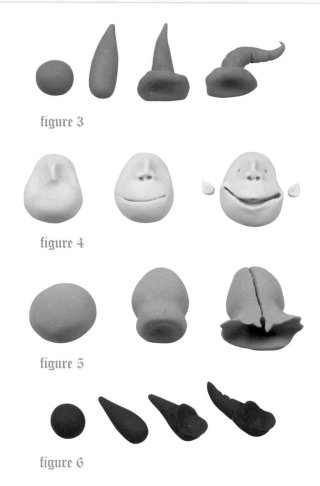

figure 3

figure 4

figure 5

figure 6

the rounded end and gently draw the edges up and out. Mark creases over the top of the shoe with the marking tool and twist the tip of the shoe upwards (Figure 6). Repeat to make a second shoe. Roll out a little yellow modeling paste and cut a strip for the belt. With the bit of orange modeling paste you set aside earlier, roll a small ball to form the buckle and flatten into a disk.

3. To assemble the figure, insert a wooden skewer into each leg of the pants, leaving enough extending from the top to provide support through to the head and enough extending from the bottom to reach the shoes and firmly into the cake. Press the shoes onto the bottoms of the skewers. Press the shirt onto the tops of the skewers and affix the belt, buckle, and straps across the shirt seam. Insert two toothpicks horizontally into the shirt, one into each shoulder, and press on the sleeves, cuffs, and hands. Press the collar and face onto the skewers and affix the eyes, eyebrows, hair, and hat. Set aside to dry for six hours.

Bushels of golden straw

4. Roll about 2 oz (57 g) of yellow modeling paste into a thick cylinder. Narrow the cylinder a little near both ends and mark lines lengthwise all around the cylinder with the marking tool, defining the straws. Press in the cylinder at both ends with your finger and trim the edges in a jagged fashion with the sharp knife. Roll two very thin sausages of yellow modeling paste and wrap them several times around the narrower parts at either end of the cylinder. Repeat to make five more bushels of golden straw and set aside to dry for 30 minutes. Mix the gold luster powder with a little water and paint the bushels, making sure to paint inside the ends as well (Figure 7). Set aside to dry for three hours.

figure 7

Cake and cake board

5. Level the cake with the serrated knife and turn it upside down onto a flat surface. Spread buttercream generously on the top and sides with the rubber spatula. Roll out the white rolled fondant and wrap the cake, trimming the edges with the pizza cutter. Transfer to the cake board and position in the middle. To make the wall around the side of the cake, thickly roll out 19 oz (538 g) of light gray modeling paste. Cut with the pizza cutter to make two rectangles, each measuring 3 x 14.5 inches (7.6 x 37 cm). Roll each piece horizontally with the brick-textured rolling pin. With the sharp knife, follow the outline of the bricks along one long edge of each piece, cutting out bricks to make an uneven top for the walls. Affix around the cake with the textured sides facing outwards.

Finishing touches

6. Carefully remove the dried wall from the rim of the baking pan and affix on top of the cake with royal icing. Support with pieces of sponge until dry, at least three hours. With the dark gray, black, and remaining light gray modeling paste, shape about 35 rocks of various sizes and shapes, and affix on top of the cake. Affix Rumpelstiltskin near the wall by pressing in the skewers extending from his shoes. Affix four bundles of straw on top of the rocks and the other two bundles of straw on the cake board. Set aside to dry for six hours.

Remove all non-edible supports
before serving the cake.

The Three Little Pigs

 **hree little pigs went out into the world to seek their fortunes.** The first pig built a house of straw. The second pig built a house of wood. The third pig built a house of bricks. A wily wolf knocked on the door of the first pig's house and said, "Let me in!" "No, no, no!" replied the pig, "Not by the hair of my chinny chin chin!" "Then I'll huff, and I'll puff, and I'll blow the house down!" said the wolf—and he did. The wolf proceeded to the second pig's house. After a similar exchange there, he blew that house down, too. The wolf then proceeded to the third pig's house, but things were a little different there. The wolf huffed, and he puffed, but he couldn't blow the house down! So the wolf wandered off, and the pigs lived in peace in their sturdy brick house.

Materials

2 lb 11½ oz (1.2 kg) modeling paste (page 12), divided and tinted to make:

   12¾ oz (312 g) yellow

   3 oz (85 g) light brown

   3 oz (85 g) dark brown

   7 oz (198 g) reddish brown

   4½ oz (127 g) skin color

   ¼ oz (7 g) pink

   1¾ oz (49 g) orange

   1¾ oz (49 g) dark blue

   1¾ oz (49 g) light blue

   1½ oz (42 g) green

   3½ oz (100 g) red

   1 tsp (5 ml) CMC

6 lb 10 oz (3 kg) rolled fondant (page 12), divided and tinted to make:

   2 lb 2 oz (963 g) green

   4 lb 8 oz (2 kg) white

Three 8-inch (20.5 cm) round cake boards

Three 6 x 3-inch (15.4 x 7.6 cm) round cakes (pages 9-10)

2 batches buttercream (page 11)

½ batch royal icing (page 13), tinted brown

½ batch royal icing (page 13), white

Brown gel food color

Tools

Small scissors

Marking tool

Rolling pin

Bark-textured rolling pin

Small sharp knife

Toothpicks

Brick-textured rolling pin

Bone tool

Dry spaghetti

Pieces of sponge

Pizza cutter

Decorating bag and tip

Serrated knife

Rubber spatula

6-inch (15.4 cm) cake round or plate

Instructions

Straw, wood planks, and bricks

1. To make a bushel of straw, roll 2 oz (57 g) of yellow modeling paste into a thick cylinder. Narrow the cylinder a little near both ends and press in at both ends with your fingers. Trim the edges in a jagged fashion with the sharp scissors and mark lines lengthwise all around the cylinder with the marking tool. Roll two very thin sausages of yellow modeling paste and wrap them several times around the narrower parts at either end of the cylinder. Repeat to make five more bushels of straw. To make the wood planks, thinly roll out the light brown modeling paste and roll over with the bark-textured rolling pin. Cut 10 planks of various widths and lengths with the sharp knife. Mark nails at the top and bottom of each plank using a toothpick. Repeat with the dark brown modeling paste to make 10 more planks of wood. To make the bricks, thickly roll out 1 oz (28 g) of reddish brown modeling paste. Roll over with the brick-textured rolling pin, then cut out 20 bricks using the brick imprint as a guide. Set aside the straw, wood planks, and bricks to dry for six hours (Figure 1).

figure 1

Pigs

2. To make the pig with the planks of wood, first shape a head by rolling 1 oz (28 g) of skin color modeling paste into a thick triangle with rounded corners. Draw one flat side of the triangle

upwards to form a snout. With the sharp knife, make a horizontal cut along the bottom third of the snout to form a mouth. Deepen the cut and widen it in the middle by pressing in the bone tool. With a toothpick, draw the mouth upwards at either end to form a smile. Add a small sausage of pink modeling paste to form a bottom lip, and press a little pink modeling paste onto the tip of the snout. With a toothpick, mark nostrils in the snout and eyes above the snout. Add two small sausages of skin color modeling paste for the eyebrows. Shape two small triangles of skin color modeling paste for the ears, indent with the bone tool, and affix onto the head (Figure 2). To make the pants, roll 1½ oz (42 g) of orange modeling paste into a thick, rounded square. With the marking tool, mark a horizontal line near the top

figure 2

to distinguish the waist. Shape pant legs along the bottom by drawing out the modeling paste on either side. Indent the bottom opening of each pant leg with the bone tool to make room for where the legs will go. Mark creases around the pant legs with the marking tool. To make the shirt, roll ½ oz (14 g) of yellow modeling paste into a half ball. Divide ¼ oz (7 g) of yellow modeling paste in half and shape each half into a cone for the sleeves. Indent the wider end of each sleeve with the bone tool. To make a bow tie, roll a small ball of orange modeling paste, flatten with your fingers, and cut out a small wedge. To make arms, roll ¼ oz (7 g) of skin color modeling paste into a thin cylinder and cut in half widthwise. Bend at the elbows and make a small cut at one end to form the hoofs. Make the legs in a similar manner, but with a slightly shorter, fatter cylinder. Twist a tiny sausage of skin color modeling paste for the tail (Figure 3). Assemble the pig on an elevated surface, such as an inverted cake pan. Insert a piece of dry spaghetti into the top of the pants, leaving enough extending from the top to provide support through to the head. Press on the shirt, bow tie, and head. Affix the sleeves and arms so that the arms rest on the pig's belly. Affix the feet to the pant legs and support with pieces of sponge.

3. To make the pig with the bushels of straw, use 1½ oz (42 g) of dark blue modeling paste for the pants, ½ oz (14 g) of light blue modeling paste for the shirt, and a small ball of dark blue modeling paste for the bow tie. Affix strips of green modeling paste for the suspenders and make small balls of red modeling paste indented with the bone tool for the buttons. Assemble this pig

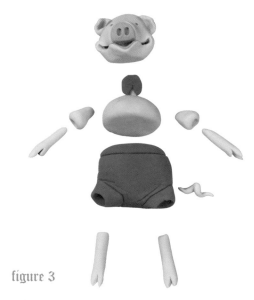

figure 3

in the same manner you assembled the pig with the planks of wood, only use a toothpick to support the upward-oriented sleeve and press the arm onto the toothpick. Position the other arm so that it rests on the belly.

4. To make the pig in the brick house, use 1½ oz (42 g) of light blue modeling paste for the pants, ½ oz (14 g) of orange modeling paste for the shirt, and a small ball of light blue modeling paste for the bow tie. There is no need to make legs or a tail for this pig, and you'll only need one arm and one sleeve. Assemble this pig on a flat surface by inserting a piece of dry spaghetti into the top of the pants and pressing on the shirt, bow tie, and head. Orient the pig so that it is leaning forward slightly. Insert a piece of spaghetti that extends horizontally at one shoulder, press on the sleeve and arm, and support with pieces of sponge. Set aside all three pigs to dry for six hours.

Brick house

5. Add the CMC to 5½ oz (155 g) of reddish brown modeling paste and thickly roll out. Cut according to the templates on page 130-131. Roll over each piece horizontally with the brick-textured rolling pin. Set aside to dry for 6 hours. To make the roof, thickly roll out the red modeling paste, cut a 4 x 4-inch (10 x 10 cm) square using the pizza cutter, then cut in half. Use the wide end of a decorating tip to press in a shingle pattern (Figure 4). Roll a thin, 4-inch sausage with the remaining ½ oz (14 g) of reddish brown modeling paste for affixing along the seam at the top of the roof. Set aside to dry for six hours.

Cakes and cake boards

6. Thinly roll out 1 lb (454 g) of green rolled fondant and cover one of the cake boards. Trim the edges with the pizza cutter and set aside to dry for three hours. Level each cake with the serrated knife and turn upside down onto a flat surface. With the rubber spatula, spread buttercream generously on the top and sides of each cake. Divide the white rolled fondant into three even parts. Roll out each part and wrap the cakes, trimming the edges with the pizza cutter. Roll out 3 oz (85 g) of green rolled fondant, place the cake round in the center, and trace around it with the sharp knife to cut out a circle. Cut a jagged edge along the circle to make a plot of grass that is just a bit smaller than the top of a cake. Repeat to make two more plots of grass and affix each plot to the top of a cake. Transfer the cakes to the cake boards and position in the middle. Divide the remaining 8 oz (227 g) of green rolled fondant into three even parts and roll each part into a

figure 4

19-inch (49 cm) sausage. Wrap a sausage around the base of each cake. Assemble the cake with the brick house on the green cake board. Position the pig inside the house with its head and arm poking out the door. Assemble the walls of the house using the brown royal icing. Support with pieces of sponge until dry, at least three hours. When the house is stable, affix the sides of the roof and the seam at the top using the brown royal icing. Make blades of grass by shaping the remaining green modeling paste into several small teardrops. Flatten the bottom of each teardrop and bend the top. Affix around the base of the house. Position the loose bricks in small piles around the house and arrange a few on the cake board. Set aside to dry for six hours. Affix the pig with the orange pants on the edge of one of the remaining cakes using a little white royal icing. Use the brown royal icing to stack 16 planks of wood, textured side up, behind the pig. Affix the remaining planks on the cake board. Affix the pig with the dark blue pants on the edge of the last cake using a little white royal icing. Affix five bushels of straw behind him and one bushel on the cake board.

*Remove all non-edible supports
before serving the cakes.*

The Nutcracker

lara was delighted by the toy nutcracker she received for Christmas,
but her brother Fritz was jealous
and broke it. The toy was mended
and placed under the tree. Later that
night, when everyone was asleep,
Clara returned to the tree to see her
beloved nutcracker and fell asleep
holding the toy. When the clock
struck midnight, she woke up—or was
she still dreaming? She found herself trapped by an army of mice!
Her nutcracker rose to defend her, slayed the Mouse King, and was
transformed into a prince. Then Clara and the prince traveled to
the Land of the Sugar Plum Fairy, where they passed a magical
evening of beautiful dances.

Materials

1 lb 4 oz (567 g) modeling paste (page 12), divided and tinted to make:

   3½ oz (100 g) yellow

   3½ oz (100 g) dark blue

   5 oz (141 g) black

   3 oz (85 g) red

   ½ oz (14 g) white

   4 oz (113 g) skin color

   Small amount of pink

   ½ oz (14 g) brown

Gold luster powder

1 batch royal icing (page 13)

9 x 3-inch (23 x 7.6 cm) round cake (pages 9-10)

1 batch buttercream (page 11)

2 lb 14 oz (1.3 kg) rolled fondant (page 12), divided and tinted to make:

   2 lb (907 g) white

   5 oz (142 g) green

   3 oz (85 g) yellow

   4 oz (113 g) red

   2 oz (57 g) black

10-inch (25 cm) round cake board

Tools

Small sharp knife

Pencil with eraser removed

Rolling pin

Small, medium, and large star cutters

Fine paintbrush

Marking tool

Bone tool

Small round cutter

Wooden skewer

Decorating bag and tip

Serrated knife

Rubber spatula

Pizza cutter

9-inch (23 cm) cake round or plate

Instructions

Gold accessories

1. Prepare the gold accessories first, as the figure is assembled only once they are dry. To make a shoulder pad, shape ½ oz (14 g) of yellow modeling paste into a ball and flatten into a wedge. Draw one side of the wide end downwards and make small vertical lines using the back of the small sharp knife (Figure 1). Repeat to make a second shoulder pad. To make the top of the hat, roll ¼ oz (7 g) of yellow modeling paste into a half ball. To make ropes for the front of the jacket, twist together two thin sausages of yellow modeling paste, cut in half, and make a gentle curve in the middle of each half. Roll a small ball of yellow modeling paste for the belt buckle, flatten, and mark with a circle using the top of a pencil with the eraser removed. Thickly roll out 2 oz (57 g) of yellow modeling paste and cut 20 stars of various sizes using the star cutters (Figure 2). Set aside all pieces to dry for 30 minutes. Mix the gold luster powder with a little water and paint all the accessories (Figure 3). Set aside to dry for three hours.

Body

2. To make the pants, roll the dark blue modeling paste into a short cylinder and flatten slightly on the front and back. With the marking tool, mark a line down the middle of the cylinder to separate the pant legs. To make the boots, roll 3 oz (85 g) of black modeling paste into a short sausage the same width as one pant leg.

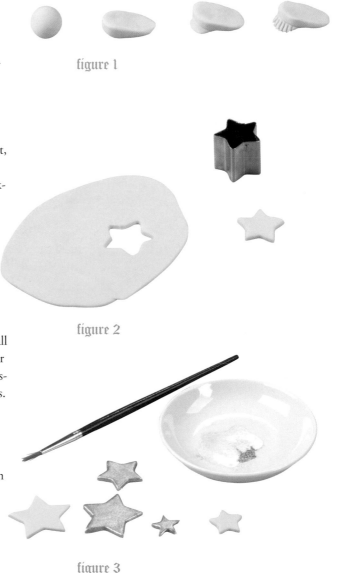

figure 1

figure 2

figure 3

Cut the sausage in half widthwise. Bend each half at a 90° angle to form an ankle and flatten the bottom. Mark creases on the front using the back of the knife. Roll out a little black modeling paste and cut two thin strips for the boot cuffs and a thinner, longer strip for the belt. Make the jacket by rolling 2½ oz (71 g) of red modeling paste into a thick cylinder. Cut out a triangular section at the top for the collar. Roll out a small piece of white modeling paste and cut out a triangle to fit into the collar space. Thinly roll out a little red modeling paste and cut two thin strips to make sleeve cuffs. Set aside a little red modeling paste (for the bottom lip) and divide the rest in half for the sleeves. Shape each half into a cylinder that is as long as the jacket body. To make gloves, roll two small balls of white modeling paste and flatten slightly. With the sharp knife, separate the thumb and make shallow cuts to mark fingers. Roll another small ball of white modeling paste and flatten to make the neck. Shape a small square of white modeling paste to affix at the back of the head (Figure 4).

Head

3. Set aside a little skin color modeling paste (for the eyelids and nose) and roll the rest into a ball. Make two indentations with the bone tool for the eye sockets. For the jaw, mark three lines at the bottom of the ball with the sharp knife. Thinly roll out a little white modeling paste, cut a small rectangle, and mark teeth with the sharp knife. To make the eyes, roll two small balls of white modeling paste and flatten into disks. Roll two smaller balls of black modeling paste and flatten into disks. Roll some black modeling paste into two

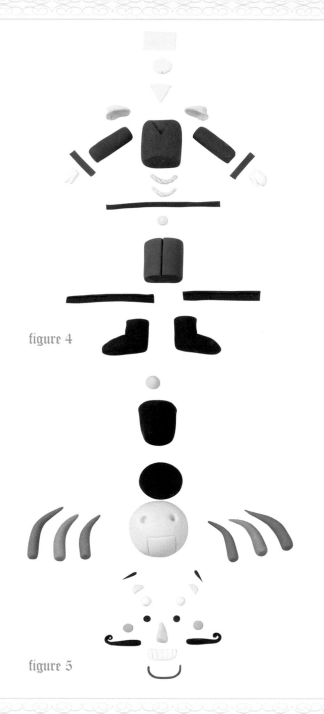

figure 4

figure 5

114

elongated teardrops and flatten for the eyebrows. With the skin color modeling paste you set aside, shape two small crescents for the eyelids and a cone for the nose. Roll the red modeling paste you set aside into a thin sausage for the bottom lip. To make a mustache, roll a little black modeling paste into two very elongated teardrops and curl the narrower ends upwards to spiral around themselves. Roll two small balls with the pink modeling paste and flatten into disks for cheeks. Roll several sausages with one tapered end out of brown modeling paste for the hair. To make the hat, roll 1½ oz (42 g) of black modeling paste into a cylinder with one end slightly wider than the other. Roll out ¼ oz (7 g) of black modeling paste and cut with the round cutter to make the base of the hat (Figure 5).

4. To assemble the figure, insert a wooden skewer through the middle of the legs, leaving enough extending from the top to provide support through to the head and enough extending from the bottom to press through a boot and into the cake. Wrap the cuffs around the top of the boots and affix the boots at the bottom of the legs. Press the jacket onto the top of the skewer and affix the belt around the waist. Affix the cuffs around the bottom of the sleeves, then affix the sleeves, gloves, belt buckle, collar, ropes, and shoulder pads. Use the royal icing to affix the gold pieces. Press on the neck and head and affix the teeth, lip, cheeks, mustache, nose, eyes, eyelids, and eyebrows. Affix the hair all around the head, then affix the top hat and the gold half-ball. Set aside to dry for six hours.

Cake and cake board

5. Level the cake with the serrated knife and turn it upside down onto a flat surface. Spread buttercream generously on the top and sides with the rubber spatula. Roll out the white rolled fondant and wrap the cake, trimming the edges with the pizza cutter. Transfer to the cake board and position in the middle. Roll out the green rolled fondant, place the cake round in the middle, and trace around it with the sharp knife to cut out a circle. Affix on top of the cake. Thinly roll out the yellow rolled fondant and cut out strips measuring ½ x 4 inches (1.3 x 10 cm). Affix the strips all around the side of the cake so that they form Vs. Set aside to dry for 30 minutes. Mix some gold luster powder with a little water and paint the strips, taking care not to get any gold paint on the cake. Set aside to dry for three hours. Thinly roll out the red rolled fondant to a 1½ x 29-inch (3.8 x 74 cm) rectangle and cut in half lengthwise to make two strips, each measuring ¾ x 29 inches (1.9 x 74 cm). Affix one strip around the bottom of the cake and the other around the top. Roll the black rolled fondant into a thin, 29-inch (74 cm) sausage and wrap around the top of the cake, at the seam between the green base and the upper red strip. Position the Nutcracker exactly in the middle of the cake (you may want to measure with a ruler to be sure) and insert the skewer extending from the bottom of the figure deep into the cake. Affix the golden stars on top of the cake and set aside to dry for three hours.

Remove all non-edible supports before serving the cake.

Thumbelina

 **humbelina was a tiny girl born of a lovely flower.** Beautiful and petite, she was carried away by a frog who wanted Thumbelina to marry her son. Thumbelina escaped the betrothal thanks to a helpful butterfly. But a mayfly quickly arrived and whisked Thumbelina away again. When the mayfly abandoned her, a field mouse helped her out. But the mouse planned a wedding between Thumbelina and a mole. A bird saved Thumbelina from that fate and placed her in a field of flowers. Here, Thumbelina met the Prince of Fairies—a match that suited Thumbelina just fine. They were soon married and lived happily ever after.

Materials

4 tsp (20 ml) CMC

1 lb 3½ oz (555 g) modeling paste (page 12), divided and tinted to make:

    3½ oz (100 g) light pink

    3½ oz (100 g) medium pink

    3½ oz (100 g) dark pink

    4 oz (113 g) green

    2½ oz (71 g) skin color

    1½ oz (42 g) orange

    1 oz (28 g) dark brown

Blue and red gel food color

4 lb 12 oz (2.2 kg) rolled fondant (page 12), divided and tinted to make:

    1 lb 14 oz (850 g) blue

    2 lb 6 oz (1.1 kg) white

    8 oz (227 g) purple

    2 oz (57 g) yellow

12 x 12-inch (30.5 cm) square cake board

10 x 10 x 2-inch (25 x 25 x 5 cm) square cake (pages 9-10)

1 batch buttercream (page 11)

1 batch royal icing (page 13)

Tools

Rolling pin

Large leaf cutter

Leaf veiner

Small leaf cutter

84 2-inch (5 cm) pieces floral wire

Wooden rods (such as rolling pins), or paper tubes made by rolling ordinary white paper and taping it up along the seam

Small sharp knife

Toothpick

Dry spaghetti

Fine paintbrush

Spiral-textured rolling pin

Pizza cutter

Serrated knife

Rubber spatula

9-inch (23 cm) cake round or plate

Weave-textured rolling pin

Decorating bag and tip

Instructions

Petals and leaves

1. Add 1 tsp (5 ml) of CMC to the light pink modeling paste to make it particularly stiff. Thinly roll out and cut out 14 petals using the large leaf cutter. Lay each petal on the leaf veiner and press gently to indent (Figure 1). Add 1 tsp (5 ml) of CMC each to the medium and dark pink modeling paste, roll out, cut out 15 medium pink petals and 15 dark pink petals with the large leaf cutter, and vein each petal. To make the leaves, add the remaining CMC to the green modeling paste and thinly roll out. Cut 40 leaves using the small leaf cutter and vein each leaf with the leaf veiner. Lay a piece of floral wire on the veined side of all 84 petals and leaves, at the bottom. Pinch the modeling paste over the wire and press the sides together. Wrap all of the pieces backwards (smooth side down) around wooden rods or homemade paper tubes so that they take on a gentle curve (Figure 2). Set aside to dry for six hours.

figure 1

Thumbelina

2. Prepare the legs by rolling 1 oz (28 g) of skin color modeling paste into a thin sausage and folding in half. Narrow gently toward the tips of the sausage to create the contours of calves, pinch in a little to form ankles, and flatten the tips to shape feet. Bend the folded end of the sausage up and back so that the figure is in a kneeling position (Figure 3). To make the dress, roll the orange modeling paste into a rounded

figure 2

cone. Form a waist by narrowing the cone about three-quarters of the way up from the bottom and press in the neckline to make room for the neck. Press in the bottom of the cone to create an opening for the legs and pull the edges outward to shape a flared skirt. Roll ½ oz (14 g) of skin color modeling paste into a thin sausage and cut in half widthwise to make two arms. Bend at the elbows and flatten at one end to form hands. With the sharp knife, separate the thumb and make shallow cuts to mark fingers. Roll ⅔ oz (19 g) of skin color modeling paste into an egg shape for the head. Add a small ball of skin color modeling paste for the nose and mark eyes with a toothpick. Roll ⅓ oz (9 g) of skin color modeling paste into a cone for the neck and flatten at the chest end to fit into the neckline of the dress. With the dark brown modeling paste, roll several sausages for the hair (Figure 4).

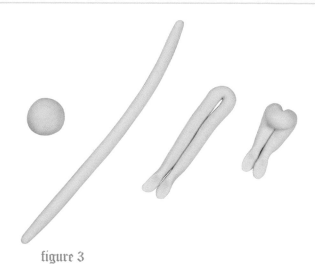

figure 3

3. To assemble the figure, insert a piece of dry spaghetti into the top of the legs, leaving enough extending from the top to provide support through to the head. Press the dress onto the spaghetti and affix the arms, arranging them so that they rest on the lap. Press on the neck and head and affix the hair. Paint on facial features with the gel food color.

Cake and cake board

4. Thinly roll out 1 lb 8 oz (680 g) of blue rolled fondant and cover the cake board. Roll with the spiral-textured rolling pin, then trim the edges with the pizza cutter. Set aside to dry for three hours. Level the cake with the serrated knife and turn it upside down onto a flat surface. Spread

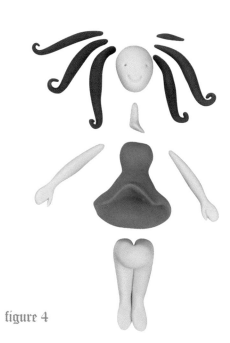

figure 4

buttercream generously on the top and sides with the rubber spatula. Roll out 2 lb (907 g) of the white rolled fondant and wrap the cake, trimming the edges with the pizza cutter. Transfer to the cake board and position in the middle. Roll the purple rolled fondant into a 36-inch (92 cm) sausage and affix around the base of the cake. Roll out the remaining blue rolled fondant to slightly larger than a 9-inch (23 cm) circle and roll with the spiral-textured rolling pin (Figure 5). Place the cake round in the middle and trace around it with the sharp knife to cut out a circle. Position on top of the cake, textured side up. To make the flower center, shape the remaining white rolled fondant into a large half ball. Thinly roll out the yellow rolled fondant, roll with the weave-textured rolling pin, and lay over the half ball. Trim the edges with the pizza cutter (Figure 6).

figure 5

5. Affix Thumbelina to the middle of the flower center using a little royal icing, then affix the flower center in the middle of the cake. Arrange the light pink petals in a ring around the flower center by inserting the floral wire extending from the bottom of each petal firmly into the cake. Make a ring of the medium pink petals next, then an outer ring of dark pink petals. Arrange the leaves in a similar manner around the edge of the blue circle on top of the cake. Set aside to dry for three hours.

Remove all non-edible supports before serving the cake.

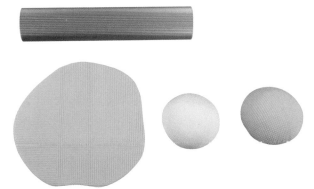

figure 6

Templates

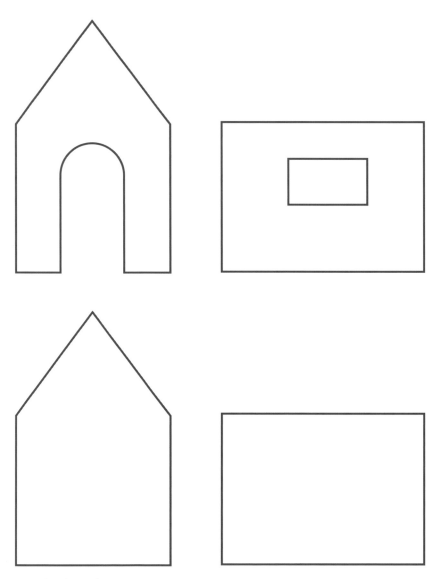

Hansel and Gretel

Hansel and Gretel

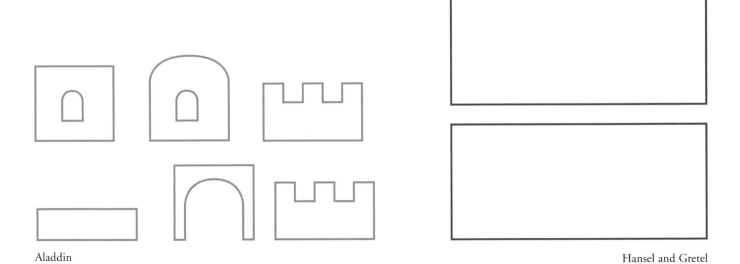

Aladdin

Hansel and Gretel

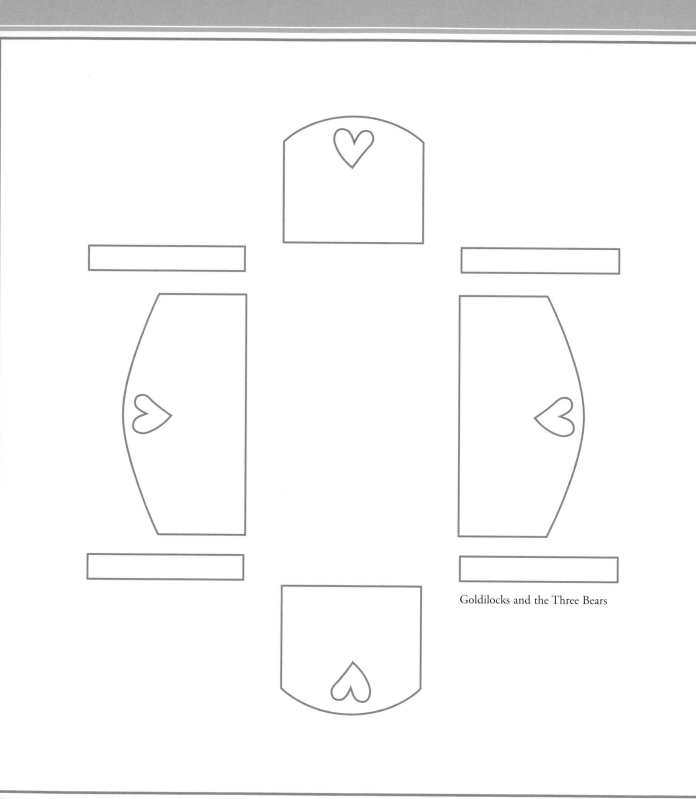

Goldilocks and the Three Bears

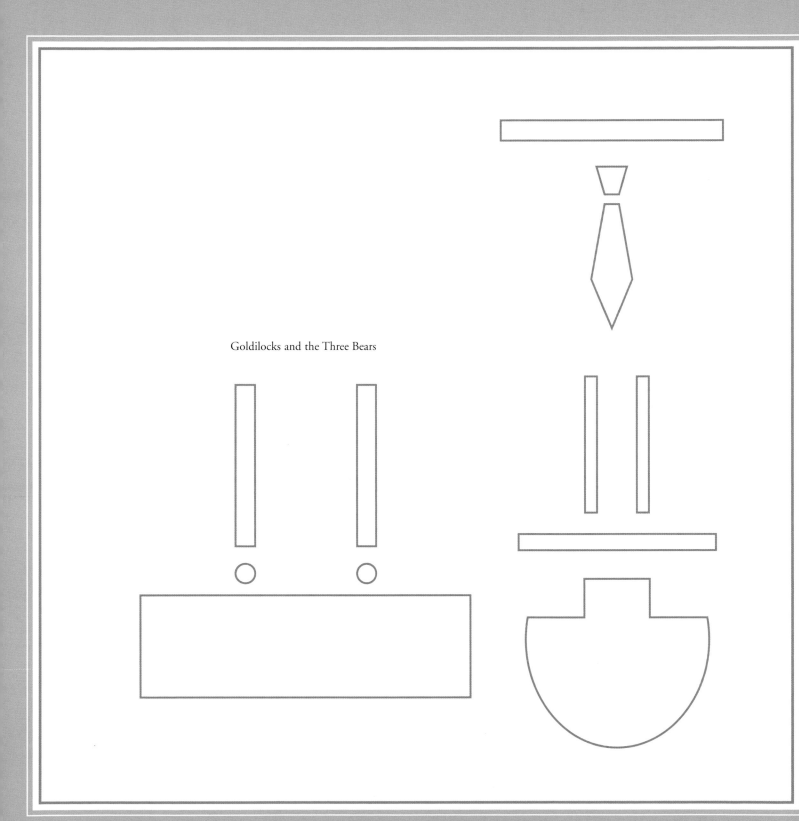

Goldilocks and the Three Bears

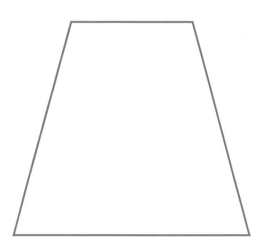

Cinderella

Pinocchio

Puss in Boots

Snow Queen

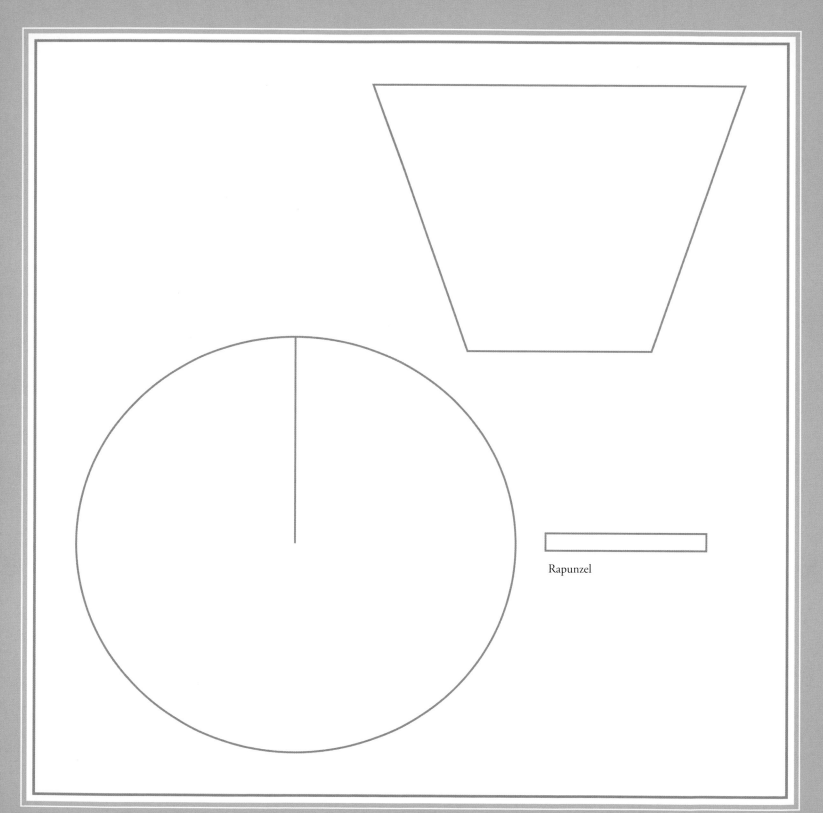

Rapunzel

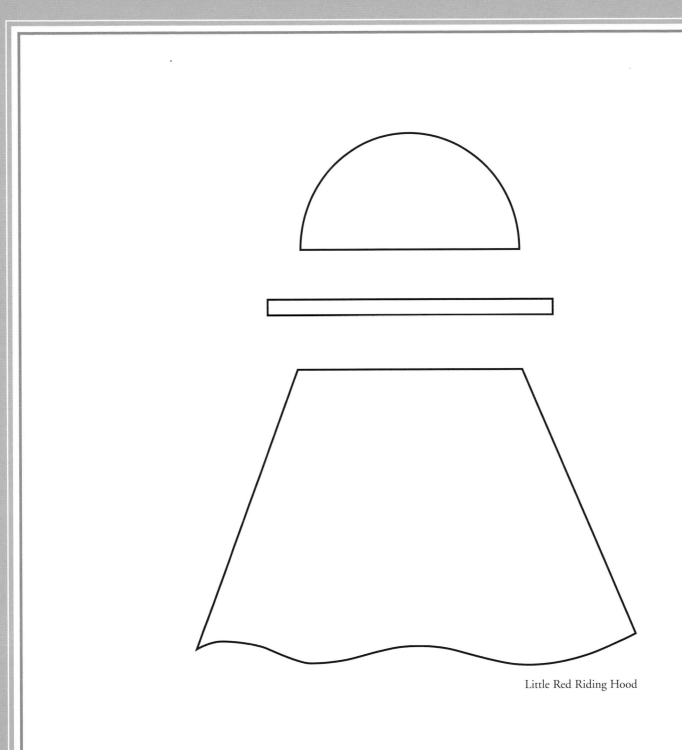

Little Red Riding Hood

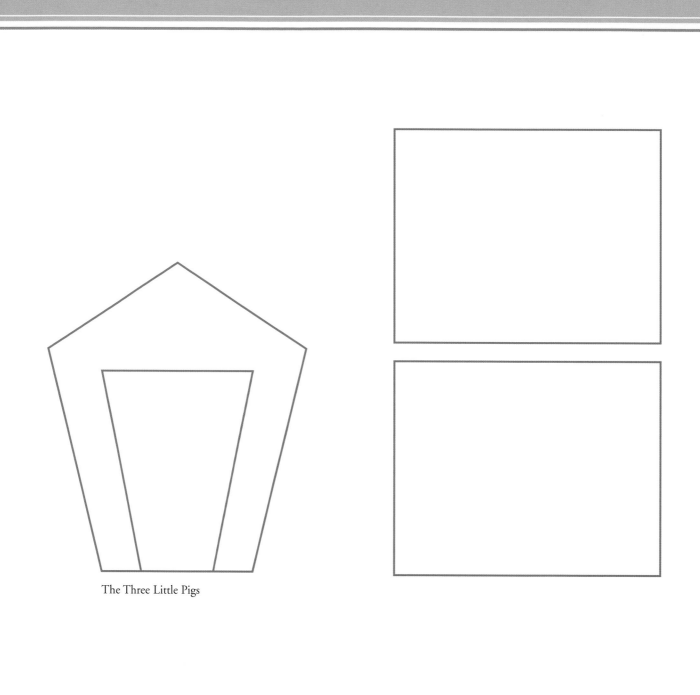

The Three Little Pigs

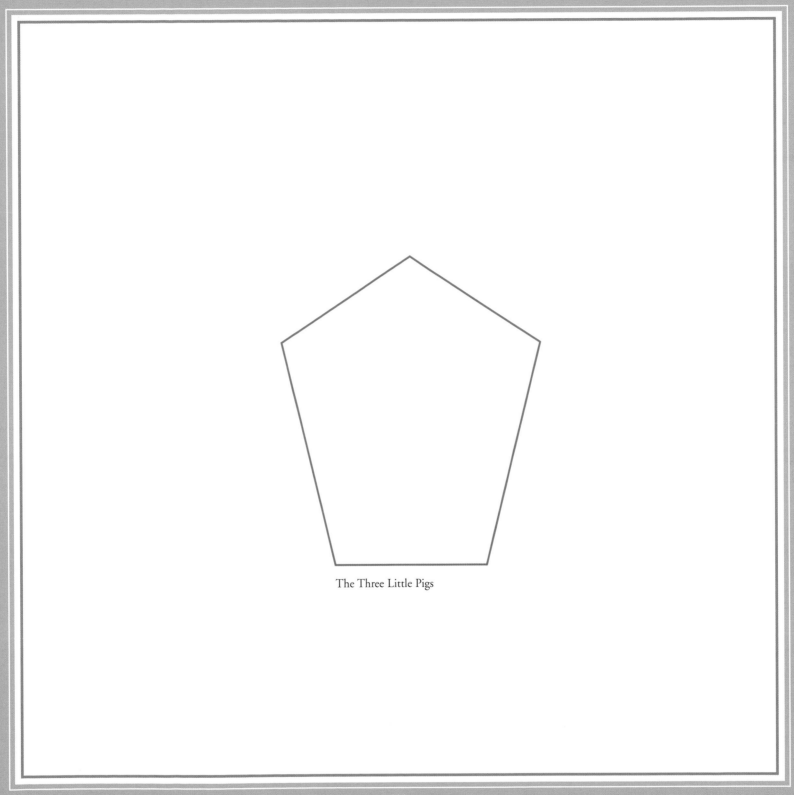

The Three Little Pigs

Index